# Becoming a Filmmaker: Making it in London's Film Scene

Krish Pinto

Copyright © 2025

All Rights Reserved

ISBN:

# Table of Contents

Dedication ................................................................... x
Acknowledgment ......................................................... xi
About the Author ........................................................ xii
Preface ..................................................................... xiv
Introduction ................................................................. 1
What This Book's About................................................ 1
Who It's For ................................................................. 4
What You Can Expect................................................... 5
What You Should Take Away ....................................... 7
Chapter 1 - Fuck… What Did I Get Into? ....................... 9
My initial love for filmmaking ......................................... 9
Making sense of what I liked and why ......................... 11
How I would start out if I were starting out .................. 16
Step 1: Watch with Purpose ........................................ 16
Step 2: Research the Roles ........................................ 17
Step 3: Test the Waters Online ................................... 17
Step 4: Get on a Set ................................................... 18
Step 5: Talk to the Pros ............................................... 19
Step 6: Pick and Commit ............................................. 20
Why This Works.......................................................... 20
Learning from Films .................................................... 21
1. FOUNDATIONAL CLASSICS (To understand film grammar & visual storytelling) ................................... 21
2. CINEMATOGRAPHY-DRIVEN MASTERPIECES (To study light, texture, and camera) ............................. 22
3. MINIMALISM & MICRO-BUDGET INSPIRATION (For indie filmmakers & stylized realism) ....................... 23

4. BOLD STYLE + DIRECTORIAL VOICE (Learn how vision shapes everything) .................................................................. 24

5. Linear Narrative Structure ................................................ 25

6. Unique NARRATIVE STRUCTURE & CONCEPTUAL IDEAS (For storytelling craft + unique voice - films that break the norm) 25

Learning from books ............................................................ 26

1. Rebel Without a Crew by Robert Rodriguez ........................ 26

2. In the Blink of an Eye by Walter Murch ............................... 27

3. Making Movies by Sidney Lumet ....................................... 27

4. The Filmmaker's Handbook by Steven Ascher & Edward Pincus ........................................................................................... 28

5. Directing Actors by Judith Weston ..................................... 29

Why These Books Matter Now .............................................. 31

The Shift ................................................................................ 31

First few weeks in the London Film Industry ......................... 32

Learnings from Film School .................................................. 35

Film School Gave Me a Toolkit - Not a Ticket ....................... 35

Learning the Language of Cinema (One Department at a Time). 35

Real Gear. Real People. Real Chaos. .................................. 38

The Truth: Film School Isn't Magic. It's a Mirror. .................. 39

Attempts on gaining experience in the Industry .................... 40

The reality after graduation .................................................. 43

Reshaping my mindset ......................................................... 45

Learning from rejection ......................................................... 49

Chapter 1: Advice ................................................................. 53

Bluff Boldly, Then Learn Fast ............................................... 53

Start Anywhere, Just Start .................................................... 54

Hunt Jobs Where Crews Hang ............................................. 54

Pack for Survival ................................................................... 54

Embrace the Grind ........................................................................ 55
Lean on experienced crews ......................................................... 55
Watch Everything, Steal Smart ..................................................... 55
Rethink Rejection .......................................................................... 55
Master the Small Stuff ................................................................... 56
Own Your Outsider Edge .............................................................. 56
Chapter 2 - Production – The Great Indian Jugaad ..................... 57
Team, Locations, Catering, Gear, Transport. ............................... 60
Step 1: Master Patience ................................................................ 66
Scene One: The Van That Never Came ....................................... 68
Step 2: Ditch the Short Temper .................................................... 70
Step 3: Hone Persuasion .............................................................. 75
Step 4: Communicate Effectively .................................................. 78
Step 5: Put It All Together ............................................................. 80
Why This Works ............................................................................ 81
How to get work in Production ...................................................... 88
The Hustle: Going the Extra Mile .................................................. 89
Challenges for Newcomers ........................................................... 91
The Importance of Location .......................................................... 92
Persistence Pays Off .................................................................... 92
LinkedIn: Connecting with a Purpose ........................................... 93
Building Meaningful Connections .................................................. 94
Film Festivals and Events: The Best Networking Grounds .......... 95
Making Sense of the Chaos: Staying Persistent .......................... 96
Conclusion: Persistence, Strategy, and Meaningful Connections 97
Chapter 3 - Riding the Waves – Employment Shifts in the UK Film Industry ......................................................................................... 98
The industry from 2020 to 2025 ................................................. 100

Global Influence and Cultural Impact ........................................... 104
Unexpected Detail: Tax Incentives ............................................... 105
Unexpected Detail: Studio Space Edge ........................................ 105
Findings: ............................................................................................. 105
Graph Placeholder 1: Employment Boom (2020-2022) ............. 106
Graph Placeholder 2: Employment Rollercoaster (2023-2025) . 108
The future of the film industry - Where do we see it going? ....... 108
Jobs: Growth with a Catch ............................................................. 109
AI's Grip on London's Film Future ................................................ 110
Spending: Cash Keeps Flowing ..................................................... 111
Reflection: Making Sense of the Madness .................................. 112
The Conundrum: Chasing Dreams Through Side Gigs ............. 113
Chapter 4 -The Camera's Eye – Learning the Craft .................. 120
Building up my cinematography portfolio .................................. 123
First Frames: Man in the Mirror ..................................................... 124
Actionable Lessons: What My Stumbles Teach You ................. 125
Lesson 1: Reading Light - What to Check and Where to Point.. 129
Lesson 2: Calculating Lighting Ratios ........................................... 130
Lesson 3: Ditch the Monitor - Know Your Camera ..................... 131
Lesson 4: Lighting a Scene - Start with Blocking ........................ 132
Key Takeaways: What I Learned from the Grind ....................... 133
1.It Starts with Wanting to See, Not Just Shoot .......................... 133
2. Gear's Just a Tool Know It Inside Out ..................................... 134
3. Simple Stories Build Your Eye .................................................. 134
4. Question Every Frame Thanks, Sudeep .................................. 135
5. Light Meters Are Your TruthZac's Gospel ............................... 135
6. Ratios Set the VibeDial It In ....................................................... 135
7. Trust Your Camera, Skip the Screen ....................................... 136

8. Blocking Your Blueprint Light Later.......................................... 136
9. Sun's BossWork Around It....................................................... 136
10. Stumbles Are Your Guru......................................................... 137
Why It Matters.................................................................................. 137
How to Enter the Camera Department and Climb to the Top: A Cinematographer's Playbook.................................................... 137
The Entry Point - How to Get Your First Camera Gig ................. 138
Entering the camera department ................................................. 141
1. Learn How to Build a Camera from Scratch ......................... 143
2. Understand Camera Accessories and Why They Matter....... 145
3. Know How to Prep Like a Pro ................................................ 146
4. Learn Exposure and Monitoring Tools ................................... 147
5. Match Your Technical Skills to the Story .............................. 148
Start Shooting - The Only Way to Get Noticed ........................... 149
Getting Seen: How to Show Your Work and Get Booked........... 150
Shoot. Share. Repeat. .................................................................. 151
The key: Consistency over virality. Keep showing up................. 152
2. Make a Showreel That Actually Hits ..................................... 152
3. Your Network Is Your Net Worth............................................ 153
4. Get Credited Everywhere....................................................... 154
5. Use Downtime Strategically ................................................... 155
Climbing the Ladder – 1st AC to DP ............................................ 156
Timeline to Becoming a Top-Tier DP (And Staying There)........ 157
Influences: ...................................................................................... 158
1.    The Fall (2006) – DOP: Colin Watkinson ...................... 158
Composition & Camera Movement .............................................. 159
Colour & Texture............................................................................ 159
2.    Enter the Void (2009) – DOP: Benoît Debie ................... 160

Camera Movement & Unusual Shots ................................ 160
Lighting & Color .................................................... 161
3. The Duke of Burgundy (2014) – DOP: Nikos Aliagas ........... 161
Composition & Framing .............................................. 162
Lighting & Atmosphere .............................................. 162
4. The Holy Mountain (1973) – DOP: Alejandro Jodorowsky .... 163
Composition & Symbolism ........................................... 163
Color & Lighting .................................................... 163
5. A Ghost Story (2017) – DOP: Andrew Droz Palermo ........... 164
Composition & Camera Movement .................................... 164
Lighting & Atmosphere .............................................. 165
Final Thoughts ...................................................... 165
1. Have your own kit of unique camera toys. ................... 166
2. You remember the grad film I shot, "The Other Brother." ..... 166
3. Remember that every frame counts .......................... 167
The Future of Cinematography ...................................... 167
Understanding the New Tools ....................................... 169
From Set to Simulation ............................................. 170
The Rise of the Hybrid Cinematographer ........................... 171
Lighting the Unreal ................................................ 172
Case Study — Dune .................................................. 173
When the LED Wall Becomes a Location ............................. 174
The New Language of Previz ........................................ 174
What This Means for You ........................................... 175
Chapter 5 - The Future of Film and where It's heading ........... 177
Silent Film & the Invention of Visual Language (1910s–1920s) 179
The Sound Revolution (1930s–1950s) ............................... 180
Colour, Scope, and the Spectacle (1950s–1960s) .................. 181

The Auteur Era (1970s–1980s) .................................................. 182
Digital, Indie, and DIY (1990s–2000s) ........................................ 183
Streaming, Social Media & the Fragmentation of Cinema (2010s–Now) ................................................................................ 184
The gameplan: ........................................................................... 191
Pick a Platform - But Know What It's For .................................. 193
Show, Don't Sell ........................................................................ 193
The Content Loop (That Doesn't Burn You Out) ....................... 194
Growing Beyond the Screen ...................................................... 195
Luck, Timing, and Staying Sane ................................................ 196
Here's what's in your control: .................................................... 196
Interview Section ....................................................................... 200
The change being made in Production Companies ................... 206
1. AI in Scriptwriting and Pre-Production .................................. 209
2. AI in Post-Production ............................................................ 211
Case Studies ............................................................................. 213
Chapter 6 - Coming to a close .................................................. 214
Bibliography .............................................................................. 216
Books & Essays ........................................................................ 216
Industry Guides / UK-Specific .................................................. 217
Articles & Whitepapers ............................................................. 217
Podcasts .................................................................................... 217
Websites & Platforms ............................................................... 218

# Dedication

For those who don't know where to start or feel lost, this one's for you.

# Acknowledgment

This book wouldn't exist without the community that helped me survive my first few years in the film industry. To my mentors, friends, and crewmates, thank you for sharing your wisdom, your gear, and your late-night wrap beers.

To all the authors who helped me compile this together over the years.
A special thank you to the runners, assistants, and behind-the-scenes heroes who rarely get the credit they deserve; you kept things moving even when the cameras weren't rolling.

To my family for letting me chase this wild dream. And to every person who said, "You should write this down." I finally did.

To Karu & V

This one's because of you.

# About the Author

Note: Please write loosely based on this - Feel free to edit where necessary. The focus is to subtly convey that I am more of an author than a filmmaker, and I write books.

Krish Pinto is a writer first, an author who fell in love with words before falling in love with cameras. For him, storytelling started on the page: scribbled scripts, half-finished book ideas, and journal entries between shoots. Writing became the one constant in a chaotic industry, a way to make sense of what it means to create, survive, and grow in film.

Krish is also a filmmaker and creative producer based in London of Indian and Portuguese heritage. He has worked his way through the industry from the ground up, from early call times as a runner to high-pressure sets as a production coordinator and camera trainee.

His work spans commercials, music videos, and narrative projects, but whether he's behind a camera or a keyboard, Krish is always chasing the same thing: stories that move people.

Becoming a Filmmaker is his first book that delves deep into personal anecdotes and statistics about the London Film Industry.

He wrote it as a love letter to the underdogs trying to break in and a reminder that your voice matters, even if no one's handed you a mic.

This is his first but not his last.

# Preface

Four years. That's how long I've been navigating the labyrinthine world of filmmaking in London. Four years of early mornings, late nights, unpredictable schedules, and the constant hum of anticipation and uncertainty. Four years filled with more rejection emails than I care to remember, yet equally infused with moments of pure, unadulterated joy and accomplishment.

This book isn't a glossy, idealized portrayal of the industry. It's not a guide filled with easy answers or quick fixes. Instead, it's a raw, honest account of my personal journey, the triumphs and tribulations, the highs and lows. It's a testament to the sheer perseverance required to find your footing in a fiercely competitive landscape. I've avoided the temptation to offer definitive career advice; every path in filmmaking is unique. My goal is not to present a formula for success but rather to share the lessons I've learned, the hurdles I've overcome, and the unexpected joys I've encountered along the way. Through relatable anecdotes and honest reflections, I aim to provide a realistic glimpse behind the curtain, shedding light on the realities of working on film sets in one of the world's most vibrant film capitals.

I hope this journey resonates with aspiring filmmakers, giving them a sense of what to expect, preparing them for the challenges, and inspiring them to pursue their passions, even when the odds seem stacked against them. Consider this book a companion for the journey, a testament to the resilience required, and a celebration of the collaborative spirit that makes filmmaking such a unique and rewarding experience. My hope is that readers will not only gain insights into the practicalities of the industry but also find inspiration in the power of perseverance, the importance of collaboration, and the inherent magic of cinematic storytelling. Through all of the crazy stories, there's something that keeps all of us creatives alive, that indescribable feeling that I attempt to make sense of.

"I dream for a living" - Steven Spielberg.

# Introduction

## What This Book's About

Imagine a young man from Bombay, cradled by the cacophony of street vendors and the flicker of cinema screens, stepping into London's relentless drizzle with nothing but a dream to craft films. That's me - your guide through this unvarnished chronicle of ambition, adversity, and art. This book is not a sanitized memoir or a prescriptive blueprint to fame; I'm not here to speak down to people. It ain't a shiny CV or some step-by-step guide to the Oscars. It's me spilling the truth about chasing a lens when you've got no connections, no cash, just a gut full of hunger. It is a vivid excavation into the United Kingdom's film industry from the perspective of someone who is currently hurdling through.

The allure of London's film industry is undeniable. The city pulses with creative energy - a vibrant, unpredictable symphony scored by decades of cinematic triumphs, underground movements, and every scrappy student film in between. It's a place where you can brush shoulders with Oscar winners on the Northern Line, where a random East End alleyway becomes a set for a streaming giant, and where even the rain sometimes looks like it was lit on purpose.

For many, the idea of making it in London's film scene feels like the ultimate dream - an intoxicating mix of red carpets, BBC offices, wrap parties, and high-profile premieres. The promise glimmers in all directions: the chance to be part of something meaningful, to create art, to tell stories that reach people.

But step behind the lens-not figuratively, but quite literally - and things look different.

After being thrown into the deep end of this world, I quickly discovered a truth that no glossy behind-the-scenes featurette can capture. Beneath the glamour, the tuxedos, and the glamorous job titles lies a reality far more complicated, demanding, and often unglamorous. You don't see the cold, unpaid 6 a.m. call times in Zone 5. You don't see the exhaustion behind that one "perfect" take. And you definitely don't see the quiet panic of your camera card corrupting mid-shoot. (We'll get to that story.)

This book distills my journey from an outsider with no foothold to a filmmaker carving a niche amid the industry's chaos. It lays bare the hidden costs of chasing a vision: the side gigs that erode your pride, the solitary nights wrestling with self-doubt, and the fleeting triumphs that whisper of possibility. Through my lens, you'll witness the industry's pulse - its cyclical booms and busts, its gatekeepers and rebels - without drowning in arcane data. Yet this is more than a personal tale; it's a meditation on the universal pursuit of creative purpose in a world that often demands conformity over courage. I offer no rose-tinted myths, only truths - scarred, human, and laced with the spice of my Bombay roots.

This book is not a victory lap. It's not a highlight reel. It's more like a personal field report - rough-edged, honest, and still unfolding. It offers a firsthand perspective of what it's really like to build a film career in one of the world's most competitive creative hubs. And spoiler alert: my journey was not a straight line. It was crooked, chaotic, and sometimes completely unplanned.

My path wasn't the kind they turn into a feel-good montage. There were no fireworks, no overnight success stories, and definitely no smooth ascents. But this book isn't just a personal diary. It's meant to be useful - a bit of a survival kit. I'll break down the technical knowledge I picked up the hard way: camera basics, lighting setups, gear that won't break the bank, and ways to build your eye by observing how the city itself breathes light.

I also go deep on what they don't tell you: how to survive long days, how to navigate egos, how to ask for fair pay without sounding like a diva, and how to protect your creativity in an industry that can sometimes feel creatively bankrupt. This book also has a chapter on the state of the film industry in the UK and where it is going.

Don't get confused; this book isn't a data dump - let's be real, I'd rather shoot a scene than read a spreadsheet. But the UK film industry's numbers and predictions? They're the undercurrent to my story, the tides I swam as a desi outsider chasing a lens in London. I dabble in those facts and forecasts, not to flex stats, but to ground my grind in the real, showing you how the game's shifts hit dreamers like me where it hurts and where it hopes.

In 2025, the industry's a beast: studios are pumping billions, with high-end TV and films hitting record spending, fueled by tax credits and UK crews who can turn mud into magic. Forecasts say cinema's rebounding - blockbusters are pulling crowds, maybe topping a billion quid at the box office. But the crystal ball's foggy for indies: funding's tight, and small films fight for air against streaming giants. Jobs are plenty - tens of thousands - but freelancers face gaps, and whispers of AI tools spark both buzz and dread. Will they cut costs or cut us out? That's the gamble.

I weave these threads into my tale, not with jargon, but with the weight they carried - every boom a chance to climb, every slump a test of grit. You'll see me hustle through this world, where a fat budget might mean a runner's gig, but a dry spell means dal for days. It's the industry's rhythm that shaped my path from nowhere to now.

## Who It's For

If You're Just Starting Out... This book is especially for you.

For the person who's Googling "how to get a job in film with no experience,

For the one holding a light stand on a short film, wondering, Is this it?

For the fresh graduate already battling imposter syndrome.

For the outsider, the misfit, the self-taught, the passionate perfectionist who just wants to tell a good story.

You don't need to be the most talented person in the room. You just need to care. You just need to start. But it's not just for film heads. If you're grinding for any creative gig - writing songs, painting murals, building apps - this speaks to you. It's for anyone who's ditched a safety net to chase a spark, who's eaten instant noodles to stretch a quid, who's felt the weight of "maybe I'm not enough." Even if you're just curious, bingeing shows, and wondering what goes on behind the gloss, pull up. This is for dreamers, hustlers, and anyone who's ever bet on themselves, no matter the odds. You're my people - let's talk.

## What You Can Expect

The chapters ahead follow that trajectory - from my very first unpaid roles to more complex gigs in production and cinematography. From frantically running errands across South London to lighting a set on a tight schedule with three lights and a prayer. I share the highs (those rare "I belong here" moments) and the lows (technical disasters, creative blocks, awkward industry events, and an entire scene shot out of focus).

If there's one lesson that stands out, it's this: you can't do it alone. For all the talk of "networking" in this business, the truth is, it's not about shaking hands and swapping business cards - it's about making real human connections. People you laugh with on long shoots. People who back you up when things go wrong. People who believe in you before you believe in yourself.

The jobs I got, I got through people. Not algorithms. Not "exposure." Not luck. People. And many of those connections started from moments that had nothing to do with work - chatting over a sandwich, helping someone carry gear, or staying behind after wrap to help clean up. Film is a team sport; the sooner you embrace that, the stronger you get. Now, here's the unexpected twist. Somewhere along this journey - amid all the madness of shooting schedules, location dramas, and lighting diagrams - I started writing. At first, it was for myself. Notes from the set. Little reflections on what I'd learned. Sometimes rants. Sometimes gratitude lists. Over time, those scribbles turned into essays, articles, and eventually, this book.

I didn't grow up thinking I'd become a writer. But writing became the only way I could make sense of what I was experiencing. It helped me reflect, digest, and sometimes just laugh at how ridiculous things got. Then something clicked: there weren't enough honest books about starting out in the film industry. Especially not in London. Especially not from someone still in it. Most books came from the top-down, written by industry veterans looking back decades later. And while those are valuable, I felt there was space for a book written from the trenches - from someone still figuring it out.

And even more than that, I realised I wanted to help. Not in a preachy way. Not as a guru. But just as someone who's been through the same fire and can now hand you a match, a torch, or a bottle of water, depending on what you need. That's what this book is: part memoir, part manual, part message-in-a-bottle. A letter to every dreamer who wants to step behind the lens and make it out alive.

Open this book, and you're stepping into my world - no script, no filter. It's like sitting down with me at a greasy spoon, chai steaming, as I unpack my journey from Bombay's noise to London's hustle. You'll get stories that hit hard - days that broke me, days that patched me up. I'm not here to preach or polish. Expect the grit: stretching a fiver for a week, dodging rain on sets, finding my place in a game that didn't know my name.

## What You Should Take Away

Before we dive in, I want to be clear: I don't have all the answers. I'm not speaking from the top of some mountain. I'm still climbing, still making mistakes, still figuring it all out. I'm not pretending I've "made it" - I haven't. I'm just a little further ahead on the path, looking back to say, "Hey, here's what helped me - maybe it'll help you too."

I can't promise you'll direct a blockbuster by page 200. What I can give you is clarity on the grind, the game, and what's in you. This book shows the film industry for what it is: tough, flawed, rapidly evolving, but beatable if you've got heart and hustle. You just need to show up, mess up, learn, and show up again. If I can make someone feel a little less lost, a little more seen, or a little more equipped to survive their first shoot, then writing this was worth it.

So let's begin.

Let's pull back the curtain. Let's talk about the things that go wrong, the small wins that feel massive, and the quiet magic of a perfectly lit frame.

# Chapter 1 - Fuck... What Did I Get Into?

**My initial love for filmmaking**

As far back as I can remember, I've always wanted to get into filmmaking. Cheesy, but if you know that this was influenced by "Goodfellas," you're reading the right book.

Growing up, I never knew what I wanted to do in film, but I knew that I wanted to be a part of a film before it landed in theaters. Growing up in the land of Bollywood, Bombay, I was automatically reeled into cinema. My parents were traditional; they didn't want me to enter a field filled with uncertainty and, in those days, disdain. The Bollywood industry is an extremely difficult industry to survive in, and completely not for a family looking for their son to have a stable life. My parents' plan was for me to study, go to university, graduate, get a job, make them proud, get married, buy a house, have kids, and retire while in a care home.

This was a little difficult for me to digest, to say the least, but I was still young, and I had time to break the chain. Back then, I was on track for their plan for me. So, my initial years could be compared to those of Walter Mitty; I was in and out of school and film sets, drinking chai with production teams after school exams.

I was the black sheep of not only my family but also the society that I grew up in. I was born into a Christian household, and my first language was English, not Hindi, which I later learned was a massive shock to the British mates I made in London. Their faces turned red after I used to correct their grammar.

Anyway, being brought up in this unusual environment in the middle of Bombay, my influences were like a bowl of Bhel. My TV list was Breaking Bad and Two and a Half Men, while I rewatched Sholay and Gangs of Wasseypur. I loved films made by Indian auteurs in different states of India. Mani Ratnam, S. Shankar, Priyadarshan, Vetrimaaran, Anurag Kashyap. Rajesh Khanna, Rajnikanth, Amitabh Bachchan, Salman Khan, and Nawazuddin Siddiqui were frequent faces on my screen. Getting access to the internet, I learned more about International cinema. Oldboy, Memories of Murder, Project A, and Nine Queens changed my view on only watching films in languages I understand; subtitles were all that I needed. If I were to describe the films I would want to make it would be either comedies, crime/dramas and action films, or a mixture of all three. My ideal film would be Goodfellas meets Pushpa.

If you are interested in my taste in films and to get a glimpse of how I don't exactly have a favourite genre of films, here's my Letterboxd top 15:

My Top 15 of all time (Based on Preference)

Anand

Wolf of Wall Street

Goodfellas

Coda

Parasite

3 Idiots

RRR

La La Land

Pursuit of Happiness

Gully Boy

Ratatouile

Madagascar

Up

Lion

Gangs of Wasseypur

## Making sense of what I liked and why

In this period of my life, I wasn't sure what being in film actually meant; I just liked the concept of it. The only perspective I had back then was the one in front of a screen.

I had so much passion and love for the craft I was afraid that it wouldn't turn out to be what I wanted it to be. I didn't know I wanted to become a director back then. This leads me to the question of how one would go about deciding what they are drawn to within the film industry without even knowing about the roles within the industry. For me, Bollywood was all around me, and I had access to learning about what I wanted to get into. Growing up in Bombay, films weren't just something I watched - they were oxygen. Bollywood was everywhere - blaring from TVs, posters plastered on rickshaws, and songs thumping at every street corner. But it wasn't just that, it was the chaos, the color, and the sheer madness of it all that got me. More importantly, I drew closer to it because it was something I could genuinely say I was interested in and unique from other people.

I was a kid glued to the screen, watching Amitabh Bachchan growl in Deewaar, that iconic "Mere paas maa hai" line hitting like a punch. Or Rajnikanth in Sivaji, flipping coins and nonchalantly flicking chewing up into his mouth like a boss. These weren't just movies - they were events. The drama, the songs, the way a hero could dance through a fight and still win the girl, cringey, of course, staged, of course, but it always felt larger than life. It inspired.

I'd sit there, wide-eyed, thinking, "How do they do that?" Not just the stars - the whole machine behind it. The sets, the lights, the cuts, I wanted in.

Take Gangs of Wasseypur - Anurag Kashyap's raw, bloody saga. That film messed me up. It wasn't the polished Bollywood I knew; no chiffon sarees fluttering in Switzerland here. It was gritty, real like someone took a camera and ripped open a small town's guts. Nawazuddin Siddiqui's slow-burn rise, the way the frames dripped with sweat and revenge, stuck with me.

I'd replay scenes in my head, wondering how they lit those dusty alleys, how they timed that gunshot to land like a slap. It wasn't just entertainment; it was a puzzle I had to solve. That's when I started scribbling ideas, doodling shots, and dreaming of my own stories.

But Bollywood wasn't the whole game. My dad had this old DVD player, and one day, he brought home the DVD for Goodfellas. Yeah, Scorsese crashed my Bombay party.

I popped it in, and bhai, my brain exploded. The way Ray Liotta delivered his dialogues, indescribable. That voiceover pulling you into the mob's world - it was slick, tight, nothing like the three-hour songfests I knew. I must've watched it ten times, pausing to catch how they framed Tommy's rants or lit Henry's paranoia.

That's when I started seeing cinema as a craft - every shot, every cut, every shadow had a why. I realised that even films with similar stories felt different. Maybe it was the actors or the way they were shot or the songs, I didn't know what it was but I was hungry to find out.

Then the internet happened - YouTube, pirated torrents, and the works. Suddenly, I'm drowning in foreign films and subtitles. My new best mates. Oldboy - Korean madness - blew my skull open. That hallway fight, one take, brutal as hell -I rewatched it frame-by-frame, jaw dropped. How'd they choreograph that? Then Memories of Murder - Bong Joon-ho before he was Bong Joon-ho - slow, haunting, cops chasing shadows in the rain. The way it built dread without blasting music - pure genius.

And don't get me started on Project A - Jackie Chan flipping off roofs, no CGI, just guts. That mix of action and comedy, the timing, the stunts - it was Bollywood's energy but tighter, leaner. Or Nine Queens - Argentinian con game, all twists and glances, no explosions needed. I'd pause, rewind, and stare at the screen like, "How'd they pull that off?" These films weren't shouting; they were whispering, pulling you in with smarts. I'd compare them to Priyadarshan's Hera Pheri - same hustle vibe, but Nine Queens played it cool, subtle. That's when I got it: cinema's a language told differently by everyone, and I had the chance to learn every dialect.

See, Bollywood gave me the heart - those big emotions, the crowd-pleasing chaos. Think Salman Khan in Dabangg, swaggering through dust, or Rajesh Khanna crooning in Anand - it's all about the feel.

My family'd cry, laugh, and sing along, and I'd watch them, not the screen, thinking, "This is power." Films could move people, shake them up, and glue them together. That's what hooked me, the idea I could bottle that magic, make someone in a dark room feel alive. I'd mix Bollywood and Hollywood in my head, bhai. Imagine Mani Ratnam's Roja with Oldboy's edge - lush hills, yes, but a gut-punch twist. I'd sketch these mashups, scribbling on napkins, dreaming of a film that'd hit like Bollywood but bite like Scorsese or Bong. It wasn't just "cool," it was a need. I had to figure out how to make that happen, how to grab a camera and turn my mess of ideas into something real.

What really got me, though? The people behind it. Bollywood showed me crews, hundreds strong, building sets, rigging lights, making three minutes of song look effortless. I'd sneak onto local shoots after school, chai in hand, watching runners dash, gaffers yell, directors pace. It was a circus, and I wanted to be the ringmaster,r but I knew nothing of what was happening.

So that's the deal; they wired me up and flipped every switch. From Bombay's dusty cinemas to late-night torrents, it was all fuel. I'm chasing that rush, the one where you nail a shot, tell a story, and someone, somewhere, feels it. That's why I'm here, slogging it out, trying to turn this obsession into something real.

# How I would start out if I were starting out

Based on what I learned from my initial learning years, here's a clear, step-by-step plan to figure out what you're drawn to in film so you can start exploring jobs that fit, from director to sound mixer, without wasting years guessing.

**Step 1: Watch with Purpose**

Start where you're at - watching films. But don't just binge; dissect them. Pick five movies from different styles - say, a blockbuster like Dune: Part Two, an indie like Aftersun, a Bollywood hit like 3 Idiots, a Korean thriller like Parasite, and a classic like Pulp Fiction.

Watch each twice: once for fun, once to study.

Focus on one element each time - dialogue, lighting, music, editing, camera moves.

Take notes: what grabs you? Maybe it's Parasite's sneaky camera angles or smart storytelling in 3 Idiots. Write down what excites you most; those are clues to roles.

Love snappy dialogue? Screenwriting might call. Obsessed with visuals? Look at cinematography or directing. This takes a weekend, costs nothing, and starts narrowing your focus. Check streaming platforms or library DVDs to access films - most have free trials or rentals under £5. Preferably, don't pirate to support the industry.

**Step 2: Research the Roles**

Now you've got feelings - it's time to match them to jobs. The film industry has dozens of roles, but you don't need to know them all yet. Start with the big ones: director (calls the shots), producer (handles money and logistics), cinematographer (shapes visuals), editor (cuts the story), screenwriter (writes the script), sound designer (builds audio), production designer (creates sets). Google "film industry roles list" for breakdowns - sites like ScreenSkills or BFI offer free guides.

Spend an hour reading; jot down three roles tied to what you loved in Step 1. For example, if music stood out, a sound designer or composer might fit. If you liked Dune's scale, producing could be your thing. Watch YouTube videos - search "day in the life filmmaker roles" for 10-minute clips from real crews. They're raw, showing what directors or grips actually do. This step builds a shortlist without overwhelming you - aim for clarity, not a PhD.

**Step 3: Test the Waters Online**

You're curious now - good. Dip into roles without leaving your sofa. Find free resources to try them out. For screenwriting, grab

Celtx's free script software and write a five-page scene - Google "short script format" for templates. Takes a day, shows if storytelling clicks.

For directing, use your phone to shoot a one-minute video - try a dialogue or chase scene; no budget needed. Upload to Vimeo for feedback from free forums like Reddit's r/Filmmakers.

If cinematography's your jam, watch free lighting tutorials on YouTube - search "three-point lighting" and test with a lamp and your phone.

For editing, download DaVinci Resolve (free) and cut a friend's holiday clips into a one-minute story. Each test takes a weekend, max. Join X conversations - search hashtags like FilmProduction or IndieFilm for pros sharing tips. Ask questions: "What's the worst part of producing?" Real answers beat guesswork. This step lets you feel roles out; no cash or contacts are required.

**Step 4: Get on a Set**

Online's a start, but film's alive on set. Find entry-level gigs to see roles up close - runner, production assistant, anything. Check Mandy.com or ProductionHive for UK jobs; filter for "no experience." These pay £80-£150/day and need no CV - just enthusiasm. Apply to five postings; even one hit gets you in. Facebook groups are also a massive help.

Spend a day watching: how's the director leading? What's the producer fixing? Shadow a sound mixer if you can = ask them one question, like "What's your biggest challenge?" You'll see the chaos - 12-hour days, shouting, coffee runs, and what clicks for you.

If running cables feels dull but framing shots spark joy, that's data. Can't get paid work? Volunteer for student films via local university boards or Meetup groups, search "film crew London." One day on set beats weeks of theory. Log what you liked and didn't; it's shaping your path.

**Step 5: Talk to the Pros**

You've tested, watched, been on set - now talk to people doing the jobs. Find filmmakers on X or LinkedIn and search "UK film director" or "cinematographer London." Send polite, short messages: "I'm exploring film roles - can you share what a producer does daily?" Most won't reply, but one might. Aim for three chats; coffee's on you if they're local. If not, Zoom's free. Ask specifics: hours, skills, worst bits. A sound designer might say it's tech-heavy - cool if you love gear, not if you hate computers. Local film events - check Eventbrite for free screenings - put you face-to-face with crews. Chat up one person; say, "I'm new; what's editing really like?" Their answers ground your choice. This takes a week or two, builds confidence, and cuts through online noise.

**Step 6: Pick and Commit**

By now, you've got data - films, tests, set time, talks. Sit down and list your top three roles based on what fired you up. Rank them: say, director, cinematographer, screenwriter. For each, write one reason - e.g., "Directing: I love leading a vision." Pick the top one to explore first - it's not forever, just a start. Research its basics: for directing, Google "directing short films guide" and read one article (free, 10 minutes). Find a small project - write a one-page script or shoot a 30-second ad for a mate's business. Spend a month on it, under £20, with your phone. Join a free online group - Reddit's r/Screenwriting or NoFilmSchool forums to share your work. Feedback shows if it's your thing. If it's not, try your second choice. Commit to one role for three months; you'll know enough to pivot or double down.

## Why This Works

This plan is built for 2025's industry - fast, flexible, no gatekeepers. UK sets need multi-skilled folks - 21,000 new jobs by next year, says ScreenSkills, so testing roles now preps you for real gigs. It's cheap (under £50 total), takes weeks, not years, and uses free tools - YouTube, X, and your phone.

You're not picking a job for life; you're finding a spark. Maybe directing's too chaotic, but editing's your groove. Each step - watching, researching, testing, shadowing, talking, committing - builds clarity. By the end, you'll have a role to chase, skills to grow, and a network to tap. Films start with passion; this is how you turn it into a path.

## Learning from Films

Here's a list of films that I recommend anyone starting out to watch.

This list is broken into 5 categories for easier digestion:

**1. FOUNDATIONAL CLASSICS (To understand film grammar & visual storytelling)**

1. Seven Samurai (1954, dir. Akira Kurosawa)
    The blueprint for action, character arcs, and blocking.

2. The 400 Blows (1959, dir. François Truffaut)
    Humanist storytelling with documentary realism.

3. Citizen Kane (1941, dir. Orson Welles)

Every shot teaches you something about visual composition and perspective.

4. Bicycle Thieves (1948, dir. Vittorio De Sica)
Emotionally raw neorealism: how to direct non-actors and stay invisible.

5. 12 Angry Men (1957, dir. Sidney Lumet)
Masterclass in blocking and tension within one room.

## 2. CINEMATOGRAPHY-DRIVEN MASTERPIECES (To study light, texture, and camera)

1. The Assassination of Jesse James by the Coward Robert Ford (2007, dir. Andrew Dominik)
Roger Deakins's magic painterly, melancholic, unforgettable.

2. In the Mood for Love (2000, dir. Wong Kar-wai)
Lyrical pacing, color, and romantic restraint. A cinematographer's poem.

3. Children of Men (2006, dir. Alfonso Cuarón)
Bold long takes, immersive world-building, and urgent visuals.

4. The Master (2012, dir. Paul Thomas Anderson)

70mm, brutal intimacy, and performance-driven camera decisions.

5. La Haine (1995, dir. Mathieu Kassovitz)
High-contrast black & white; kinetic yet raw, full of political bite

## 3. MINIMALISM & MICRO-BUDGET INSPIRATION (For indie filmmakers & stylized realism)

1. Locke (2013, dir. Steven Knight)
Entirely in a car. One actor. Teaches control, tension, and restraint.

2. Primer (2004, dir. Shane Carruth)
Lo-fi sci-fi with a complex narrative and no hand-holding. Tiny budget, massive ideas.

3. The Fits (2015, dir. Anna Rose Holmer)
Mysterious, poetic, short, and shot like a slow-burning fever dream.

4. Krisha (2015, dir. Trey Edward Shults)
Made with family, shot in 9 days. Raw directing and emotional claustrophobia.

5. Shiva Baby (2020, dir. Emma Seligman)

One location, anxiety-infused brilliance, relatable for anyone who's ever made a short film and dreamt of scaling up.

## 4. BOLD STYLE + DIRECTORIAL VOICE (Learn how vision shapes everything)

1. Dogtooth (2009, dir. Yorgos Lanthimos)

Unnerving, absurd, but carefully controlled. Pure voice-driven cinema.

2. Run Lola Run (1998, dir. Tom Tykwer)

Editing, movement, and tension told in multiple timelines.

3. Moonlight (2016, dir. Barry Jenkins)

Lush visuals, silence, vulnerability a deeply lyrical style.

4. Under the Skin (2013, dir. Jonathan Glazer)

Experimental and strange, it blurs the line between fiction and doc.

5. Columbus (2017, dir. Kogonada)

If you love architectural composition and silence. Pure visual meditation.

## 5. Linear Narrative Structure

1. Vertigo - Alfred Hitchcock

2. The graduate

3. Parasite

4. Inside Out

## 6. Unique NARRATIVE STRUCTURE & CONCEPTUAL IDEAS (For storytelling craft + unique voice - films that break the norm)

1. Arrival (2016, dir. Denis Villeneuve)
   Sci-fi meets emotion. Narrative structure as theme.

2. Synecdoche, New York (2008, dir. Charlie Kaufman)
   Meta filmmaking that breaks rules while teaching you structure.

3. Memento (2000, dir. Christopher Nolan)
   Tells its story backwards, essential for playing with memory and narrative.

4. Eternal Sunshine of the Spotless Mind (2004, dir. Michel Gondry)

Emotion + surreal visuals + non-linear editing = directing goldmine.

5. The Lunchbox (2013, dir. Ritesh Batra)

Understated, beautiful Indian storytelling. Minimalism with soul.

## Learning from books

It wasn't only through films that I had got my initial passion for them. I was also incredibly influenced by books about filmmaking. Books can be your shortcut, not to fame, but to clarity. I've picked five that cut through the noise, each one a tool to sharpen your craft and keep you sane. These aren't dusty textbooks; they're written by people who've lived the grind - directors, editors, and insiders who know the game. They're for anyone breaking into film, from London's soundstages to indie sets in back alleys. I'm laying out why they matter, what they teach, and how they fit the 2025 hustle.

**1. Rebel Without a Crew by Robert Rodriguez**

Robert Rodriguez wrote Rebel Without a Crew in 1995, chronicling how he made El Mariachi for $7,000, a film that hit Sundance and launched his career. I read this book in my early days and remember thinking that it's a diary full of resourcefulness - how to shoot with borrowed gear, edit on a shoestring, and charm your way onto screens. It's incredibly practical. Rodriguez details practical hacks: using wheelchairs for dolly shots and cutting costs with friends as actors. In 2025, his approach resonates as budgets tighten for independents.

This book is for anyone starting with nothing - no cash, no connections. The downside? After reading it, I noticed that some tech advice is dated - digital tools have evolved - but the mindset holds. Read it to know you can start small and still make noise.

**2. In the Blink of an Eye by Walter Murch**

I was a huge fan of "Apocalypse Now" and "The Godfather," the films that Walter Murch had edited. That led me to this book that distills decades of cutting into In the Blink of an Eye. It's a concise masterclass on editing's psychology - why cuts work and how they mimic human perception. Murch explains the "rule of six," prioritizing emotion and story over technical perfection. He uses examples from his films, showing how edits shape pace and impact. In 2025, with AI editing tools like Runway gaining traction, Murch's human-first approach keeps you grounded.

**3. Making Movies by Sidney Lumet**

One of the first film books that I ever read was this one. Sidney Lumet, director of 12 Angry Men and Network, wrote Making Movies as a no-nonsense guide to directing. He walks through pre-production to release - script breakdowns, casting, set dynamics, and editing fights.

Lumet's candid about failures, like clashing with studios, and successes, like nailing jury-room tension. Directors should read this first, but producers and PAs gain from understanding a director's headspace.

Its limit? Less focus on digital-era distribution, but the craft lessons are timeless.

## 4. The Filmmaker's Handbook by Steven Ascher & Edward Pincus

The Filmmaker's Handbook is the industry's go-to manual, updated by Steven Ascher to cover digital filmmaking. Keep this book in your back pocket; if it doesn't fit, buy bigger pants.

It spans cameras, sound, lighting, editing, budgets - everything from script to premiere. It's technical but clear, with charts on codecs and tips for crowdfunding. In 2025, UK filmmakers face rising costs - £2.1 billion spent on films last year, says BFI - so its budget hacks are gold. This is for everyone: runners learning terms, producers crunching numbers, and DPs picking lenses. Its depth suits the UK's mix of big sets and scrappy shoots, where versatility is key.

Downsides? It's hefty, and some sections skim newer tech like VR. Still, it's your desk reference - my copy's battered from quick checks. Get it to speak the industry's language and avoid rookie mistakes.

**5. Directing Actors by Judith Weston**

When directing my first short film, I used this book to help me make breakdowns and, most importantly, learn the correct language to talk to actors. It taught me about "Result Direction".

Judith Weston's Directing Actors is about getting performances that breathe. Directors and producers benefit most. It's practical but lacks tech integration, a minor gap. It's a game-changer for coaxing raw takes, especially on tight schedules. Read it to make actors your allies, not obstacles.

Other Books in specific departments based on recommendations from industry colleagues.

Sound
Sound for Film and Television by Tomlinson Holman

The Practical Art of Motion Picture Sound by David Lewis Yewdall

The Sound Effects Bible by Ric Viers

Producing

The Producer's Business Handbook by John J. Lee Jr. & Rob Holt

So You Want to Be a Producer by Lawrence Turman

The Independent Film Producer's Survival Guide by Gunnar Erickson, Harris Tulchin, & Mark Halloran

Directing

Film Directing Shot by Shot by Steven D. Katz

My First Movie edited by Stephen Lowenstein

Hitchcock/Truffaut by François Truffaut

Screenwriting:

Adventures in the Screen Trade by William Goldman

Editing

The Conversations: Walter Murch and the Art of Editing Film by Michael Ondaatje

Cinematography

Cinematic Storytelling by Jennifer Van Sijll

The Five C's of Cinematography by Joseph V. Mascelli

# Why These Books Matter Now

In 2025, the UK film industry is a pressure cooker £5.6 billion in production, 126.5 million cinema admissions, yet indies and freelancers fight for scraps. These books aren't just reads; they're weapons. Rodriguez shows you how to start with nothing, vital when funding's down 22% for local TV. Murch keeps your edits sharp against AI's rise. Lumet and Weston teach leadership and empathy, critical with crew shortages loomingScreenSkills wants 21,000 new workers. Ascher's handbook arms you with tech know-how, from Arri cameras to post-production apps, saving cash and cred.

Pick these up, and you're not just learning; you're building a mindset. They cover craft (editing, directing), hustle (budgets, DIY), and people (actors, crews), aligning with the industry's demands for multi-skilled talent. They're not perfect; some lag on digital trends, but together, they're a crash course. X chatter and Goodreads reviews back their clout, with thousands of filmmakers swearing by them. Start here, and you're ahead of the pack, ready to carve your name in a game that's as tough as it is thrilling.

## The Shift

There's a certain point in every obsessed film kid's life when the obsession starts to demand more - more access, more exposure, more freedom. For me, that tipping point came when I realized Bombay wasn't enough. The film sets I was sneaking onto were thrilling, but I knew I was just orbiting the industry, never really in it. I was still the chai boy with big eyes and a bigger notebook, scribbling down lighting setups and fake shot lists.

I needed to leave to actually begin.

I was extremely eager to learn more about how films are made, and I somehow convinced my parents to ship me off to London with the guarantee that I would fend for myself after I graduate (In hindsight, I really should've thought that through). When I got accepted into Met Film School in London, I thought, "This is it. It is the beginning of the rest of my story." But I wasn't prepared for what that actually meant. London, with its cloudy skies, quiet streets, and relentless tube announcements, was a total mindfuck. I went from the deafening chaos of Dadar station to the eerie politeness of the Jubilee Line overnight. And let me tell you - nobody tells you how lonely it gets when you trade biryani for baked beans.

## First few weeks in the London Film Industry

I landed in London with a suitcase, a student visa, and a dream so big it could've filled Pinewood Studios twice over. I'd enrolled at MetFilm School, dead set on becoming the next big director -

think Scorsese with a curry obsession. I'd spent years back home sketching storyboards, watching behind-the-scenes videos on repeat, and telling anyone who'd listen I'd be calling "action!". London was my shot, my golden ticket.

What I didn't know was that the film industry here doesn't give a damn about your dreams, it's a meat grinder, and I was fresh mince.

First week at MetFilm, I'm buzzing. Classes are slick, lecturers who've shot for BBC, edit suites humming with Premiere Pro. I direct my first exercise, a two-minute short about a man losing his keys. I'm pacing the set, yelling "cut!" like I'm Kubrick reborn, and it feels electric. Then, feedback hits: "Too static," "No vision," "Where's the story?" Fair enough, I think, I'm green. I'll get better. So I pitch bigger ideas, shadow directors on student shoots, and even cut a sizzle reel. But when it's time to crew up for real projects, no one's tapping me to helm. Directors are gods here, and I'm still a mortal with a shaky iPhone short to my name.

But then, slowly, something started to shift. I started using my "otherness" as my power. While some people were busy trying to copy Spielberg's dolly zoom or Fincher's cold palettes, I was out there blending the hyper-stylised masala of Pushpa with the handheld grit of the City of God. My ideas weren't polished, but they were loud. Messy. Real.

I also began to appreciate London on its own terms. The grey skies that once depressed me started to feel cinematic. The tube became this weird metaphor for movement - always going somewhere, everyone on their own story arc. And the people? Some of the kindest, most creatively fucked-up minds I've ever met. Suddenly, I wasn't the odd one out. I was the only one bringing something different to the table. And that difference? That was gold.

But it wasn't all romantic either. There were months I couldn't afford to eat properly. For weeks, I didn't shoot anything. Days I questioned everything. Was this sacrifice - the homesickness, the debt, the mental toll - even worth it?

Turns out, yeah. Because London didn't just teach me how to make films. It taught me how to survive while making them.

I became my own crew. I learned to light a scene with fairy lights from Poundland and a bounce board made out of takeout foil. I edited entire short films on a cracked version of Premiere. I used free buses to location scout. I hustled on student sets like it was a Netflix series. I made mistakes. So many mistakes. But I kept shooting. Kept experimenting. Kept saying, screw it, let's roll. London stripped me down, and in doing so, rebuilt me.

So yeah, the transition wasn't easy. But without that cold slap of reality, without that massive leap into the unknown, I wouldn't be here. I wouldn't be this version of myself. The guy who came to London wide-eyed and overwhelmed? He's still in here somewhere, but now he's got calloused hands, cracked knuckles, and stories to tell. Real ones.

## Learnings from Film School

### Film School Gave Me a Toolkit - Not a Ticket

There are a million ways into this industry, and film school is just one of them. Some people climb in through the crew door, some people sneak in through the edit suite, and others, like me, come in through the front - paying for a student ID that says "filmmaker in training."

What MetFilm gave me is a solid foundation in filmmaking. A structure. A safe space to fail miserably and try again. And maybe most importantly, it gave me the language. The ability to speak "film" across every department.

### Learning the Language of Cinema (One Department at a Time)

At MetFilm, we weren't trained in one thing. We were thrown into everything. From the first term, it was like being tossed into the eye of a creative storm. One week, we were writing screenplays; the next, we were breaking down budgets.

It started with screenwriting - the bones of it all. Plot structure, character arcs, act breaks, motivation, and stakes. We picked apart scripts scene by scene, line by line, until we stopped seeing them as stories and started seeing them as architecture. I began to understand how a story breathes. What moves plots, what is exposition, and how to tell a story using every element of filmmaking, not just dialogue.

Then came directing, and that's where things got intense. Directing at film school is kind of like being given the keys to a Ferrari before you've passed your driving test.

You're behind the wheel, screaming with joy... until you crash it into a ditch called "underdeveloped concept." Directing taught me that having a vision is easy - executing it? That's war.

Blocking actors, motivating performances, communicating your ideas without steamrolling your crew - it's a fine art. One that I was terrible at first. But you learn fast when you're on a student set, and you've got six hours to get a four-page scene before security locks the building.

Then came cinematography - and that's when things started to click for me. I'd always had a thing for visuals, but this was the first time I really understood the science behind the magic.

We learned about lens choice, depth of field, lighting setups, and how movement affects emotion. I fell in love with the dance between light and shadow. I started watching films differently - not for the plot, but for the texture of the image, how the light in Roma felt soft and sacred, and how uncut gems moved like a panic attack. I wanted to understand how to build an emotion frame by frame. I stopped being just a director and started thinking like a DoP.

And then, there was producing. The least glamorous and most essential part of the process. Budgeting, scheduling, call sheets, legal documents, insurance, and equipment rentals. Producing taught me that making a film is 50% creativity, 50% logistics, and 100% problem-solving. It was where the idealist in me had to sit down and talk to the realist. I learned that great films die without structure. That passion projects fall apart without planning. Sometimes, the best thing you can do for your story is to make a spreadsheet.

What made all of this sink in wasn't just the classes - it was the collaboration. We weren't learning in silos. We were crewing on each other's projects.

One week, I'd be directing; the next, I'd be holding the boom pole for someone else. We'd trade jobs like Pokémon cards. I was DIT on a horror short, focus puller on a romantic drama, and 1st AD on a film that took three days to shoot a five-minute scene because the director was trying to reinvent Tarkovsky. We all had different tastes, different temperaments, different chaos - but somehow, it worked.

We learned to communicate. We learned to fight respectfully and compromise strategically. We learned that sometimes, no matter how well you plan, your SD card will corrupt, your lights will flicker, your location will fail, and your actor will show up drunk. And when that happens? You adapt. You figure it out. You roll with it. That's the real curriculum.

**Real Gear. Real People. Real Chaos.**

MetFilm wasn't just about theory. We had access to actual gear - Sony's and Arri Alexas, full lighting kits, and sound equipment. If you had a passion project and a good reason, you could book the kit, get insurance, and shoot. That freedom was rare. Most film students around the world would kill to get their hands on the equipment we could borrow on a Wednesday.

We also had access to real working professionals - not just teachers who had read the books, but people who'd actually done the work. Editors who'd cut documentaries for Netflix. Writers with credits on BBC dramas. Cinematographers who shot commercials we'd seen on TV. We could book sessions with them. Ask dumb questions. Get feedback on our rough cuts. One of them told me my framing was "accidentally beautiful," which I took as the highest compliment of my academic career.

## The Truth: Film School Isn't Magic. It's a Mirror.

But here's the twist no one tells you: film school doesn't make you a filmmaker.

You make yourself one. Film school just holds up the mirror.

And sometimes, that mirror shows you things you don't want to see. Like the fact that your story isn't as original as you thought. Or that your "vision" needs a lot more planning. Or that you're better at lighting than you are at leading. But that's the point. You go there to get humbled. To figure it out. To learn the game before you play it professionally.

I knew from the first that I needed to be actively learning to learn. This wasn't a school for passive learners. If you want specific information, you have all the access to get it.

And yeah, there were days I hated it. Days I skipped class, felt lost, and wondered if I'd wasted my time and money. Some projects didn't work, and clashing egos were brutal critiques. There was the imposter syndrome that hits when someone else's short film gets selected for a festival, and yours doesn't even export properly.

But there was growth, too. Real, hard-earned growth.

Was It Worth It?

That's the question people ask all the time: "Was film school worth it?"

Here's my answer: It depends on what you're after.

If you're looking for instant connections, red carpets, or guaranteed jobs - don't bother. You'll be disappointed. But if you're looking for a space to screw up safely, to try, fail, and recalibrate before doing it in the real world -then yeah. It can be a gift.

For me, MetFilm didn't launch my career. But it gave me the tools to build one from scratch. It didn't open every door. But it taught me how to knock better. It taught me how to find my own way to make better films through the people I met over time.

And that? That's something no YouTube tutorial can teach you.

## Attempts on gaining experience in the Industry

While learning, I also tried extremely hard to get on set. I wanted to be a director, so naturally, I looked for sets where I could be a director. Spoiler: It wasn't that easy. Reality sinks in over a £6 pint in Ealing: directing's a fortress, and I've got no ladder. Two months in, I'm still begging for a chair with "Director" on it, but the only calls I get are to hold a boom pole or fetch coffee. I'm gutted- years of dreaming, and I'm sidelined before the clapperboard snaps. So I do what any broke, stubborn film nut does: I rethink everything. If I can't direct, I'll learn the game from the ground up. Production, camera, whatever - I'll claw my way in.

It all started in my cramped studio dorm at uni, where I was scrolling Facebook groups instead of writing my essay on what I thought about Verite-styled documentaries. A post popped up - a film crew needed a gaffer for a shoot in Reading. I'd never been to Reading, and I barely knew what a gaffer did, but I was restless, broke, and itching for something real. So I typed up a reply, hyping myself as a lighting wizard with skills I didn't have, hit send, and forgot about it. Two minutes later, I got a message: "You're in. See you in an hour." I stared at my phone, half thrilled, half-terrified. I'd bluffed my way into a gig, and now I had to show up.

I borrowed train fare from my roommate and made the trek from my dorm to Reading, a two-hour ride of second-guessing and Googling "what does a gaffer do." The set was a rented warehouse on the edge of town, packed with seasoned pros who moved like they'd been born holding C-stands. I stepped off the train out of my depth, lugging a backpack and a fake-it-till-you-make-it grin. The first words I heard were, "Gaffer, grab a 16 out of the van." I froze. A 16? Was that a light? A cable? A sandwich? I nodded like I knew, then bolted to the van, praying for context clues. It was a mess of gear - coils, cases, and labels I couldn't decode. I was sunk.

Salvation came from a spark - a wiry electrician with a buzzcut and a smirk. I sidled up, dropped the act, and whispered, "Mate, I've got no clue what a 16 is." He laughed, not mean, just amused, and pointed to a 16A-13A cable tucked in a large peli case. "You're the gaffer? Ballsy." I shrugged, sheepish but relieved, and he became my lifeline. With his quiet tips - move that flag, kill that practical - I faked my way through the day, hauling lights and taping gels while the crew barked orders. I didn't nail it; I knocked over a stand once and got a glare from the DP. But I survived. The set hummed with purpose, and I felt it - the rush of shaping shadows, of being part of something alive.

By wrap, I was knackered, my hands raw from cables, my brain fried from pretending. They paid me £80 cash, and I ate chips on the train home, replaying every mistake and triumph. I'd blagged my way in, leaned on a spark's mercy, and walked out a little less clueless. That gig in Reading wasn't pretty, but it was mine - a baptism by tungsten that lit a fire I didn't know I had.

Then it snowballed. I stumble across a posting on a job board - some music video in Soho needs a dogsbody. Pay's questionable

(£50 for 12 hours), but it's a set, and I'm there. Day one, I'm lugging a C-stand through a downpour, boots soaked, arms screaming. The AD is a man named Tom with a beard like a Viking and a temper to match. "Oi, don't scratch the rig!" he barks as I trip over a cable. I'm thinking, "Fuck, what did I get into?" But then the camera rolls - a grime artist spitting bars under sodium lights - and I'm hooked. It's chaos; it's alive, and I'm part of it - even though I did nothing to contribute to what was on screen, I was happy I got to support the team.

Next week, I'm on another set - a short film in Brixton that needed a spark. Then, a promo in Shoreditch. I'm a runner every bloody day, saying yes to anything that'll take me. I got into the depth of how I went about making this happen in chapter 2.

## The reality after graduation

Graduating from MetFilm was supposed to be the start of something. I had the degree, the short films, and the showreel. I even had a half-decent IMDb credit and a folder full of feedback PDFs. But the moment I walked out of that school, it felt like I was starting from scratch. No one was lining up to give me a shot. There was no confetti, no "Welcome to the Industry" starter pack. Just me, a Google Sheet of job boards, and an inbox full of "we'll keep you on file" rejections.

I spent the first few weeks obsessively refreshing Mandy.com and Production Hive like they were lottery apps. Applied to every PA, runner, junior-anything role I could find. Most of the time, I didn't even get ghosted; I just shouted into the void. Every now and then, I'd get a bite. A day on set as a production assistant. A random corporate shoot looking for a camera trainee. I clung to each one like it was gold.

I said yes to everything. I was the guy lugging 20kg of gear up five flights of stairs because the lift was broken. The guy sweeping confetti between takes at a music video. The guy smiling through a twelve-hour shoot with no lunch break because I was just happy to be on a real set. I'd show up early, leave late, and ask a hundred questions in between.

But that hustle messes with your head. One week, you're on a dream gig with a BBC crew; the next, you're jobless, watching Final Cut tutorials in your boxers at 2 a.m. I had imposter syndrome and a constant fear that I'd be stuck in "aspiring filmmaker" limbo forever. And still, I kept going. Because every small gig, every set, every awkward coffee with someone "in the industry" added up.

Here's the first lesson I'd tattoo on every newbie's arm: London doesn't care about your CV - it cares about your hustle and how you can help a set get a job done. Job boards like Mandy or Production Base were a little helpful, but Facebook groups are gold mines.

Here's my take on how I got jobs that helped me get to the next step - pubs. The Ship in Wardour Street, The Old Blue Last - crew hang there, swapping war stories over IPAs. Buy a round, ask about shoots, and suddenly, you're on a call sheet. For day one, pack a multi-tool, a raincoat, and a spare phone charger- sets eat batteries like popcorn. Expect bollockings, cold coffee, and 14-hour days. If you can hack that, you're in.

## Reshaping my mindset

The allure of London, a city pulsating with cinematic energy, had drawn me in like a moth to a flame. I envisioned myself strolling through bustling Soho streets, effortlessly networking with industry titans, and seamlessly slipping into coveted roles on prestigious film sets. The reality, however, proved to be a far cry from this romanticized vision. My arrival in London was less a triumphant march and more a tentative tiptoe into an unfamiliar, intensely competitive [SEP]landscape.

My meticulously crafted CV, a testament to my passion and nascent skills, lay dormant in digital inboxes, gathering virtual dust. The initial wave of optimism gradually receded, replaced by a gnawing uncertainty. Rejection became a constant companion, each "no" a tiny pinprick to my inflated self-belief. I poured over industry job boards, meticulously tailoring my applications to each specific role, only to be met with the disheartening silence of unanswered emails. The sheer volume of applicants, each vying for the same limited positions, felt overwhelmingly discouraging. I questioned my skills, my choices, and even my sanity. Was I chasing a pipe dream? Was my passion misplaced? The doubt threatened to consume me, whispering insidious suggestions that I should retreat, that I wasn't cut out for this grueling pursuit.

The networking events, touted as essential gateways to the industry, were equally daunting. These gatherings, meant to foster connections, often felt more akin to social minefields. The self-assured confidence of established professionals the effortless ease with which they navigated the social landscape, felt like an insurmountable chasm. I found myself clinging to the periphery, my carefully rehearsed introductions dissolving into nervous stammerings. The fear of sounding unprepared, or worse, foolish, choked the words in my throat. I spent more time observing than participating, feeling the growing isolation of being an outsider looking in. These were not the glamorous cocktail parties of Hollywood lore; instead, these were tense, tightly packed rooms filled with people nervously vying for the attention of those in power.

However, I am inherently an extrovert and rarely felt shame; I was confident even though I was naive. My first attempts at conversation were bold and clear but usually ended with an awkward silence. Why would someone help someone who has nothing to offer? My meticulously prepared questions often felt out of place or, even worse, presumptuous. I found common ground but couldn't convert these into tangible jobs. I felt like a fraud, an imposter masquerading amongst seasoned professionals. The polished façades of success surrounding me only amplified my own insecurities, deepening my self-doubt. This early phase was about far more than just technical skills; it was a crash course in navigating social dynamics, managing rejection, and maintaining self-belief against a constant barrage of negativity.

One particularly disheartening event stands out. It was a networking evening hosted by a well-known production company. I remember the slick, minimalist space, the clinking of glasses, and the hushed, conspiratorial conversations that unfolded around me. I managed to engage in a brief conversation with a seasoned cinematographer who, despite his intimidating reputation, seemed surprisingly approachable. I remember the careful way I phrased my questions. He responded politely, offering some general advice, but the conversation felt short, superficial, and devoid of the meaningful connection I desperately craved. He excused himself shortly after, disappearing into the throng, leaving me feeling even more insignificant, more like a fly on the wall observing the inner workings of an elite world.

Yet, even amidst the constant setbacks, a stubborn refusal to surrender kept me going. I found myself clinging to the fragments of positive feedback, brief exchanges with a director who praised my enthusiasm, and an encouraging word from a fellow aspiring filmmaker. I realised that a lot of people are in the same boat as me, and all I need to do is keep going. The game is not about how well you do something but how often you can do something after being rejected. The more number of times I tried, the more number of times I found success, and this had nothing to do with what I spoke about. These small acts of affirmation, like tiny embers, fueled the flame of my determination. I realised that my initial expectations were unrealistic. The path to success wouldn't be a smooth, direct trajectory; instead, it would involve a multitude of winding paths, unforeseen obstacles, and moments of sheer, unadulterated frustration.

The process of applying for jobs involved far more than simply sending off a CV. It involved meticulous research into each company's productions, carefully crafting cover letters tailored to the specific requirements of each role, and even adapting my CV to highlight relevant skills that might otherwise be overlooked. Every application felt like a gamble, a small act of faith in the face of overwhelmingly high odds. The sheer effort required, both emotionally and mentally, was draining, but the alternative –abandoning my dream – was far more unappealing.

## Learning from rejection

Each rejection served as a harsh but valuable lesson. I learned to analyze my applications, identify areas for improvement, and hone my communication skills to better convey my abilities and aspirations. I must have sent around 300 applications.

I knew then I had to shift my mindset. From thinking in a linear manner, I started to think of ways to get to my goal with what I could offer. I learnt people valued someone who could provide value to them, not someone who is asking for favours. They want an asset, not a liability, and my mindset shifted to thinking about how I can be an asset. This very thought sparked my actions.

The early hours, the long days, and the sheer physical exertion were a far cry from the idealized image I'd previously held. I faced numerous challenges: carrying heavy equipment in all types of weather, running errands under tight deadlines, and navigating unexpected situations with limited resources. There were instances where I felt overwhelmed, exhausted, and even frustrated. But even during those moments, the persistent thrill of contributing to something creative the satisfaction of seeing the final product, kept me going. These experiences taught me invaluable lessons about the realities of the industry and the perseverance required for success.

I learned the importance of meticulous preparation, the director's detailed shot list, the meticulous planning of each scene, and the intricate choreography of the crew's movements – all aspects previously hidden from my perspective. I was no longer an observer but a cog in a machine, a small part of a larger collaborative effort.

My role involved far more than just fetching coffee and sandwiches. I assisted with equipment setup, carefully carrying fragile lights and heavy camera gear. I helped manage cables, meticulously arranging them to prevent tripping hazards and maintaining a sense of order in the chaotic environment. I learned to anticipate needs, understand the flow of the shoot, and ensuring the team had the resources they required at a moment's notice. These seemingly menial tasks were a crash course in efficiency and organisation, skills that are paramount in the fast-paced world of filmmaking.

Observing the professionals at work was a masterclass in itself. I watched as the director coaxed performances from the actors, the cinematographer meticulously framed each shot, and the sound recordist looked out for discrepancies. I witnessed firsthand the collaborative nature of the process, the seamless coordination between various departments, the dedication and passion that fueled the creative endeavor. These observations were far more valuable than any textbook could ever be. I began to understand the language of the set, the unspoken communication, and the subtle cues that guided the smooth operation of a complex production.

One particularly memorable experience involved working on a low-budget independent film shot across several locations in East London. The production team was small, tightly knit, and incredibly passionate. I was primarily tasked with assisting the production department, which meant everything from ad-hoc tasks to setting up sets. The director, a young, energetic filmmaker with a clear vision, provided valuable guidance and encouraged me to participate actively in the creative process. I learned about the importance of detail and how seemingly minor elements can contribute to the overall atmosphere and aesthetic of a film. The sound design, the color, the way the camera moves, the series of shots in the edit, every decision amounted to a different outcome. It was a puzzle that could be solved in 100 different ways to give you 100 different pictures.

The contrast between my initial expectations and the realities of the industry was stark. The romanticised image I'd held of effortlessly networking with industry giants and seamlessly slipping into high-profile roles was shattered by the realities of long hours, unpredictable schedules, and the sheer hard work involved. Yet, this hard work instilled in me a newfound respect for the filmmaking process. The small victories, the gradual acquisition of knowledge, the feeling of contributing to something creative these were the rewards that kept me going.

Another crucial aspect was developing a professional attitude, which involved not only technical skills but also soft skills. This meant being punctual, reliable, and respectful of my fellow crew members. It meant being adaptable to unforeseen circumstances, anticipating needs, and offering assistance without being asked. These qualities, often overlooked in the initial stages, are crucial for building strong working relationships, fostering a sense of collaboration, and ultimately, securing further work.

The unpaid roles served as an invaluable training ground. They taught me the unspoken rules, the etiquette, and the dynamics of a film set. I learned the importance of teamwork, the value of collaboration, and the satisfaction of seeing a project through from inception to completion. The initial frustration of constantly seeking work slowly transformed into a deeper appreciation for the process, the learning curve, and the gradual accretion of skills and knowledge.

As I progressed, I realised that networking isn't merely about collecting business cards; it's about building genuine relationships, fostering trust, and establishing a reputation for professionalism and reliability. I actively engaged in conversations, listened attentively, and sought out mentors who could guide my path. These connections provided invaluable insights, support, and opportunities, helping me secure more substantial roles. Each connection, however small, contributed to my understanding of the industry and my position within it.

After countless sets and exploring, I honed down on what drew me to making films - production and camera. I liked production because the department was involved right from inception to distribution. I liked the camera and lighting because I wanted to contribute more to the creative side of filmmaking. I loved how subtle nuances in lighting and camera shaped stories, and that was something I wanted to control.

The next step was to ignore other roles and focus on getting better in these two departments.

## Chapter 1: Advice

By now, you must have understood that if you really want to get into filmmaking, I hope I haven't scared you off already. There are good parts, I promise. If you think filmmaking is just the glam and red carpets and immediate fame, this isn't for you. If you really want to tell a story and will do anything to get that chance, keep reading.

**Bluff Boldly, Then Learn Fast**

Don't be afraid to say yes to a role like that gaffer gig in Reading, even if you're clueless. Confidence can get you in the door; hustle and quick learning keep you there. Google on the train, lean on a crewmate and fake it 'til you make it. This won't work every time, but a long shot teaches you more than a calculated careful move.

**Start Anywhere, Just Start**

You don't need to direct day one. Fetch coffee, haul gear, hold a Boom - every gig, even a runner's, is a foot in the door. I used to make the best chai on set with ginger; the crews' loved it; they kept getting me back and then, eventually, stepped up.

**Hunt Jobs Where Crews Hang**

Skip the stale job boards - Facebook groups and pub chats is where it's really at (The Ship, The Old Blue Last) are where real gigs hide. Buy a pint, ask about shoots, and watch call sheets roll in. Networking's less about suits and more about pints. Note: If you don't drink, a ginger beer in a pint glass does the job just fine.

**Pack for Survival**

Day one on set? Bring a multi-tool, raincoat, and spare power bank. London sets are brutal, and gear dies fast. You never know when you'll be put up in a hotel, so carry an extra pair of clothes. I learned this while lugging C-stands through Soho rain. Be the rookie who's ready.

**Embrace the Grind**

Expect 14-hour days, cold coffee, and bollockings from ADs named Tom. My first music video was chaos - wet boots, sore arms - but the buzz of a rolling camera made it worth it. Grit gets you through.

**Lean on experienced crews**

Find a crewmate - like that electrician in reading - who'll show you the ropes. Admit what you don't know, and they'll save your arse. Collaboration is how you grow, do not aim to be a solo genius.

**Watch Everything, Steal Smart**

From Goodfellas to Gangs of Wasseypur, Oldboy to Pushpa - consume films wide and deep. I'm not suggesting you should like these films, but discover your own likes. Subtitles opened my world; mix influences into your own brew. My dream's a Bollywood re-imagined Scorsese flick – find yours.

**Rethink Rejection**

London's a meat grinder - my CV gathered dust, my pitches flopped. I learnt that getting a "no" is more common than a "yes", strive for 100 "no's". I guarantee that you will get at least 1 "yes".

Each "no" stings, but it's a lesson. Tweak your approach, not your dream. I went from begging to direct to thriving on the ground.

**Master the Small Stuff**

Runner gigs taught me workflow - how sets work, how pros think. Carrying gear in Brixton or taping cables in Shoreditch built skills that directing dreams can't touch. Nail the basics; the big breaks follow.

**Own Your Outsider Edge**

Black sheep of Bombay, English-first in a Hindi world - I turned quirks into fuel. London didn't care about my roots, just my hustle. Your weird mix of Breaking Bad and Rajnikanth? That's your voice- use it.

# Chapter 2 - Production – The Great Indian Jugaad

So, I'd survived the runner phase - wet shoes, aching arms, and a growing itch for the madness of film sets. Doing everything to learn more to be on more sets. Directing was still a dream dangling out of reach, locked behind some invisible London gate, but I wasn't about to pack my bags and head back to India. I knew that I wanted to focus on Production and Camera. This chapter covers my experience in the Production department and what I did to learn more and gain experience on sets.

Back home, we've got this thing called jugaad - making magic out of nothing, like fixing a scooter with a rubber band or stretching one roti to feed three cousins. That's what I brought to production. If I couldn't shout "action!" I'd make sure the whole show happened - sets, food, crew, everything. This chapter's about that plunge - running around like a headless chicken, producing my first short, "The Grandmaster," with my mate Saj Mirpuri, crafting a graduation film out of sand and grit, and later wrangling a beast like Lucifer 2. It's messy, it's absurd, and it's where I learned that films don't always need cash-they need hustle, heart, and a bit of desi spice.

The runner's life had already given me a crash course: say yes, show up, don't drop the gear. I was still at MetFilm, nodding through lectures when I wasn't on set. I applied my lessons out there - music videos, shorts, anything that'd take a guy with zero credits and a big grin. I'd gone from fetching teas to fetching everything - cables, lights, and egos.

One day, I'm in Hackney, hauling sandbags for a student shoot, the air thick with diesel and damp. The producer frazzled woman named Priya, a name that felt like home, catches me as I'm stacking the last bag. "Can you stay late?" she asks, eyes darting to her clipboard. "We need someone to lock up." I nod, too tired to think, and suddenly, I'm not just the runner - I'm the guy with the keys, jingling them like a prize. That's how it creeps in: one extra task, one late night, and you're in production before you know it.

Another gig, I'm in Camden, taping cables for a music video under a sky-spitting rain. The AD-a wiry guy with a buzzcut-yells, "We're missing a prop! Cricket bat, now!" A cricket bat? In London? I sprint to a charity shop two streets over, the bell jingling as I burst in, breathless. "Got a bat?" I pant. The old lady behind the counter digs out a chipped wooden one, £30. I haggle it to £ 20, my instincts kicking; I run back, handing it over like it's the World Cup trophy. The director grins, the shot rolls, and I've saved the day. Small wins, big steps. Another time, I'm in Brixton, holding a reflector for a short film about a lost dog. The DOP's swearing at the clouds- too grey, too flat- and I'm trembling, arms burning, praying I don't drop it. We get the take, a soft close-up of the pup's eyes, and the crew claps. Not for me, but I feel it, a tiny spark of the magic.

These may feel so insignificant thinking about it now, but when I was alone in my room, not knowing how to get on set, just being on set was a massive victory. Also, a side discussion is that everyone in the film industry is a little bit psychotic. We have to be otherwise; we would never last. We tune ourselves to believe the pessimistic to be optimistic; we see the world through our own rose-tinted lens. Whatever it takes to get there.

Anyway, then came "The Grandmaster." Me and Saj Mirpuri, my MetFilm partner in crime, cooked up this wild idea in our first year over lukewarm tea in the canteen. We wanted a South Indian action flick - think KGF meets John Wick- but shot with Western polish, a 15-minute short punching way above its weight. We made a deal: we would produce each other's short film. I would direct - he would produce, and he would direct - I would produce. Through this experiment, we'd prove you don't need crores to make something epic. Easy, right? Yes, but it takes a lot of effort.

Money was the first wall we smashed into. As students, we had about as much budget as a roadside chai stall- barely enough for a roll of gaffer tape. But I learned from runner days that no cash just means more creativity. We sat in my Ealing flat, the radiator humming, munching Parle-G biscuits, and broke it into five pieces.

## Team, Locations, Catering, Gear, Transport.

Crack those, and we'd have a film.

The team was a breeze. MetFilm was a treasure chest- students dying to crew up, and legally, we didn't have to pay them minimum wage. Harsh, I know, but when you're broke, you grab what you can. I roped in classmates- camera geeks who'd debate lenses like it was a cricket match, sound nerds with mics dangling from their bags, actors hungry for a reel to show their mums. When we ran short, I tapped my growing London network of runners I'd met over cold coffees, a grip from a Brixton shoot who'd nodded at my hustle. We ended up with 24 people, a mix of students and pros, like a ragtag IPL team ready to bat on a cracked pitch. I'd stand in the middle of Saj's cluttered flat, calling out roles -"You, sound! You, lights!"- feeling like a captain rallying a misfit squad.

Locations? No fancy studios for us. We'd shoot in Saj's flat, piles of laundry shoved under the bed, park with dog walkers gawking, an alley stinking of bins. Production design was our secret weapon- curtains became temple walls, a £3 rug from a market turned into a dusty floor... One night, we're in that alley, setting up a fight scene, and a drunk guy stumbles by, shouting, "Oi, is this Bollywood?" We laugh, shoo him off, and keep rolling. London's chaos became our backdrop.

Catering nearly broke me, though. Food's the silent budget-killer. London prices in 2022? A decent meal was £6 -10 times 24 crew, times four days, that's £900 we didn't have. Back home, my mum would've fed the whole mohalla for less, tossing in extra rotis for the kids. Here, we were on our own. So, I said, "Enough, we'll cook." Saj and I hit Morrison's, the fluorescent lights buzzing overhead, and loaded the biggest trolley they'd ever seen - rice, lentils, spices, chicken, onions till we couldn't see over the top - £200 in total. The cashier squinted at us, two teenagers with a mountain of groceries. "You own a restaurant?" she asked, scanning a sack of basmati. "Nah," I grinned, "just feeding a film crew." We hauled it back to my flat- two buses, arms screaming- and I turned into a one-man dhaba.

For three nights, I cooked 100 meals, packed them in Tupperware I'd begged from a neighbor. Chicken curry with cumin sizzling in the pan, dal bubbling like a monsoon puddle, rotis flipped on a borrowed tawa. The flat smelled like a spice market, turmeric, coriander, and a hint of burnt garlic when I zoned out. I burned a pan, scorched my thumb, and my fingers smelled of haldi for a week, but the crew devoured it.

First day on set, I'm handing out boxes, steam rising, and a sound guy- big beard, bigger appetite- says, "Mate, this is better than Pret." High praise for £2 a head. Lesson one: Cook in bulk, save pounds, win hearts. The crew worked harder, stomachs full, and I felt like my mum, feeding the village.

Gear was simple- MetFilm let us borrow cameras, lights, and mics for free, a perk I milked dry. Transport, though? A total nightmare. Film kits' heavy and awkward - tripods and lights that won't fit in a cab, cables tangling like a bad hair day. We couldn't afford vans, so we used a trolley-yes, a shopping trolley- dragging it through London streets, wheels wobbling under the weight. One day, we're crossing a busy road in Hackney, cars honking, and the trolley tips- tennis balls rolling, me diving to catch them. A passerby laughs, "You lot making a comedy?" "Something like that," I mutter, dusting off a Sachtler Tripod. Another time, we needed a crash mat for a fight scene. No budget, no mat. I looked at Saj, he looked at me, and we hauled my king-size bed from my flat to the set-two buses, one near-miss with a cyclist. Crew laughed as we towed it, but when the hero punched a goon and he landed soft, they clapped. Jugaad, bhai - pure Indian magic.

The Grandmaster was chaos, but it came together. Four days, no sleep, and a million fixes. One day, the lead actor twisted his ankle, no stunt double, no time- so we rewrote the scene on the spot, him limping heroically instead of leaping. The end product? A wild Action with heart and a message about grit. We screened it at MetFilm, the room packed with classmates, and people cheered loudly, real cheers. No crores, no A-listers, just us and our hustle. It taught me that films don't always need money- they need madness you can mold.

Looking back on this production, I wouldn't recommend anyone to go through what we did on this production. We pulled it off, sure, and the cheers at the end proved it wasn't a total disaster, but the bruises and turmeric-stained fingers? Not a path I'd wish on anyone. The real insight I want to share isn't about copying that chaos but what it taught me. Before you toss an idea out the window because it feels too expensive, pause, rethink it. How can you do it with nothing? How can you get creative and dodge the overheads that choke most films? That's where the magic lives, and it's a lesson worth more than a crore. Whenever I approach a low-budget film, I segregate my budget into the money that will show on screen and overheads. You can't skimp on all overheads, respect your crew, and you will get a good product. Really think about how you can maximize what goes on screen.

Take our experience. We had a vision - a big, bold story that screamed for action, heart, and a world we couldn't afford. Studios, catering, transport - those words alone could've killed it. Overheads loomed like monsoon clouds, ready to drown us. But instead of scrapping it, we flipped the script. No cash? No problem. We raided what we had - classmates became crew, a flat became a set, a £3 rug turned concrete into dust. Creativity didn't just save us; it made the film.

The point isn't to mimic that grind - please don't burn your kitchen down or tow your bed across town. It's about the mindset. Big-budget films lean on cash for polish; we leaned on hustle for soul. Before you say "too expensive," ask: How can I make this happen? Wouldn't trade the scars, but you don't need them. Rethink the "impossible" with nothing, and you'll find it's not just doable - it's better. Our film hit hard not despite the lack, but because of it. Strip the fat, get creative, and watch your vision breathe.

The film was good for a student short - gritty, bold, a story that landed - but it lacked some nuance we didn't see till later. Creativity and hustle got us far, but the cracks showed where cash might've smoothed things.

Here's the lesson: you can rival a high-budget short with basics and vision, but knowing your technical limits - and pushing past them - is what sharpens you.

Take the shoot itself. We had MetFilm's gear - a Sony FS7, some lights, mics - but we were green. One day, the fan for the camera died mid-take, a faint buzz fading to silence; we had to work around that in situations. Sound? We had nerds with mics, but in that stinky alley, a drunk guy screaming bled into the mix - charming, sure, but sloppy. Lighting was my weak spot back then - I'd barely grasped a light meter then, and Saj's flat scenes looked flat, shadows mushy where a pro rig could've carved depth. The gaffer was fresh and learning, so the film's look wasn't polished. The fight scene? My bed cushioned the fall, but shaky handheld shots and a limping rewrite hid our lack of choreography finesse. It was raw, not refined - good, not great. There were tons of errors in post-production that we couldn't fix.

Yet, we learned heaps. That fan fix taught me gear isn't sacred - improvise, adapt, keep rolling. The sound bleed? Next time, I'd scout quieter spots or sweet-talk the drunk away - location matters. Lighting flops pushed me to study ratios, not just wing it - basics I'd ignored till they mattered. The rewrite showed storytelling trumps polish - a limp-sold grit better than a leap we couldn't nail.

Technically, we were rough, but the gaps lit a fire. We didn't need crores - just more know-how. The Grandmaster wasn't flawless, but it was ours, and those cheers? They came from the heart, not nuance. Don't copy our stumbles; see this: creativity fills holes, rule-breaking buys time, and learning your craft turns good into epic, budget or not.

In this period, I found my love for writing books, I started writing a lot, drafts, screenplays, and eventually this book that has been in the works for quite a long while.

Producing is a mixture of being a smart businessman and understanding how a film set runs from the bottom up. If you can strike the right balance between these, you're on your way to becoming a great producer. Take A24 as a production company; they started by buying projects to distribute them, then started producing nice indie films. They found a gap in the industry and boosted it with creative films, which worked.

Producing a film is like running a circus - you're juggling egos, deadlines, and disasters, and if your head's not on straight, it all crashes. The production department demands a specific personality, and it's not about charm or swagger. It's built on four pillars: patience, keeping your cool, persuasion, and talking the talk right. These traits aren't just nice-to-haves; they're what separate a producer who delivers from one who flops.

In the 2025 UK film industry, where indies fight for scraps and big sets churn fast, you need this mix to turn chaos into a finished film. From what I have observed and learned, here's how to build and use these skills, step by step, so you can walk onto any set ready to lead.

## Step 1: Master Patience

Patience is your foundation - films take months, sometimes years, and nothing moves as fast as you want. Crews miss deadlines, actors flake, and permit stalls. A good producer waits without losing focus. Start small: Practice waiting calmly in daily life. Stand, breathe, and think through your day. Takes five minutes to build discipline. Apply it to work: Volunteer for a student film via Meetup (free, search "film crew [city]"). You'll face delays - gear's late, shots drag. Instead of stressing, note the issue and plan a fix, like rescheduling lunch. Takes one shoot day and shows you can handle hold-ups.

Looking back at shoots I've been a part of, patience is everything; you're always waiting for someone or something.

Waiting for the actor to show up.
Waiting for the light to shift.
Waiting for the sound to roll.
Waiting for the fog machine to warm up, even though it was "meant" to be warming up two hours ago.

It's not glamorous. It's not fun. But it's real. If you can't be patient, this industry will eat you alive.

And I didn't understand that until I was standing in a forest at 5 a.m. with wet socks, a moody lead actor, and a DOP who'd just realized we didn't bring the correct ND filters. That was the day I learned patience wasn't just a virtue - it was a survival skill.

## Scene One: The Van That Never Came

We were shooting a student short in North London. Nothing fancy, just a five-minute thriller set in an abandoned factory. We'd booked a van to bring our gear from the university's kit room to the location at 7:00 a.m. The first shot was meant to be up by 9:00.

Cut to: the van driver bailed. No backup. No gear. It's now 8:45 a.m., and we're standing in the rain, holding takeaway coffee cups and trying not to panic.

I watched the producer - a quiet, no-nonsense girl called Marta - step to the side and pull out her phone. She didn't yell. She didn't cry. She just started solving. She booked two Ubers, called her friend with a car, and rerouted the shoot day. Lunch came early. The crew warmed up indoors. We lost two hours, but still made our day.

That stuck with me. Panic is loud but useless. Patience is quiet but sharp.

I wish I could say I've always been the calm, collected one on set. But there was a short film I produced in my second year at MetFilm where I let pressure override patience, and I still cringe thinking about it.

It was meant to be a simple, emotional scene: two friends sitting on a rooftop, one confessing a deep regret. We had a golden hour booked. The location was stunning. We had a killer shot list ready. But things started going sideways fast.

First, the lead actor was late - caught in traffic. Then the lav mic battery died right before taking one, and I had to run to a Tescos to grab spares. And just when we finally rolled the camera, the wind picked up and started messing with the audio.

I could feel the time slipping away. We had maybe 30 minutes of that warm sunset glow left, and I started spiraling. Instead of breathing and thinking it through, I rushed everyone. I told the sound guy to "just roll with it." I told the actors we'd fix it in post.

I told the director to cut out a few lines of dialogue to save time. Everything was about speed. We got the shots. Technically.

But when we watched the footage back? It was unusable. I couldn't blame the director because I was pressuring him. The wind ruined the sound. The performance felt stiff. The edit was choppy because there was skipped coverage.

The whole thing lacked soul because I hadn't let it breathe. Worse? The actor messaged me after, saying she'd felt rushed and couldn't really settle into the emotion of the scene. That hit me.

Because I realized that my energy had affected the whole crew, I'd let urgency turn into panic, and everyone followed my lead.

Looking back, we could've done it differently. We could've paused, taken 15 minutes to reset. Waited out the wind. Shot coverage indoors if the golden hour was gone. Rescheduled a pickup day. But at that moment, I didn't trust that patience would serve me. I chose speed and paid for it.

That film never made it to my reel. I couldn't even fix it in the post. And it taught me, the hard way that impatience is expensive. Train Patience Like a Muscle. You don't magically become calm under pressure. It's something you train yourself to be.

## Step 2: Ditch the Short Temper

Losing your rag kills trust - crews won't follow a producer who snaps. Keeping cool means absorbing stress without barking.

Practice active listening: next time, mate vents, don't interrupt or argue. Nod, ask one question, like "What's the worst bit?" Takes 10 minutes and trains you to pause.

On set, it's gold - apply as a runner on Mandy.com (£80-£150/day, no experience). When an AD yells or a prop breaks, don't react. Count to five, suggest a solution, like borrowing gear. One day on set proves you can chill when it's hectic.

I remember working on a production when the line producer never lost his calm, and everything around him was falling apart. After the shoot, I asked him how he controlled his mind to stay positive, and he told me that losing your temper never solves an issue; you're just wasting time away from solving the problem. Watch "Mickey 17" and focus on the role of Kenneth Marshall, and you'll understand exactly what I'm saying (he's not an example; more like the opposite of what you should do).

There was this one short film shoot I was coordinating - nothing big, but it had promise. The script was sharp, the director had a vision, and we'd even secured a Red camera through a friend-of-a-friend deal. I was still in my early days, green but hungry. It was one of those 48-hour race-to-the-finish kind of jobs, with barely enough time to breathe, let alone prep.

Everything that could go wrong did. The catering was late, the location owner showed up drunk and threatened to shut us down, and worst of all, our art director forgot half the props back at their flat across town. My phone was blowing up, the director was spiraling, and I was already running on two hours of sleep and vending machine Red Bulls.

Then one of the PAs - let's call him Harry - accidentally double-booked the transport van. We had to get gear to the next location, and the van was halfway across the city on a coffee run for the DOP. I snapped. Loudly. In front of everyone.

"What were you thinking, man? This is basic stuff! Use your brain!"

The set went dead quiet. Harry just stood there, blinking. The director didn't say anything, but I could feel it - the whole crew clocked the shift in the room. After that, no one really looked me in the eye. People just did what they had to, but the vibe was gone. No jokes. No trust. The entire day limped on like a body without a soul.

I apologised to Harry later, but the damage was done. We wrapped the film, sure, but I didn't get called back by that director again.

At the time, I thought, Whatever, it was just one project. But six months later? That same director was crewing up for a funded indie feature. Guess who was brought on as production manager? Harry. Guess who didn't get so much as a text? Me.

It stung. Not because I missed a gig - those come and go - but because I'd let ego trump leadership. I'd made myself the centre of the crisis instead of defusing it. I burned a bridge over a coffee run.

If that same chaos happened today- the van, the coffee, the missing gear, the ticking clock- I wouldn't lash out. Not because I've magically become this Zen monk of production, but because I've learned the hard way that your real job on set isn't just to organise; it's to lead. And leadership isn't about barking commands or solving everything yourself. It's about keeping people willing to go through the fire with you.

So now, if Harry came to me and said, "Hey, I messed up. The van's not here." I'd probably take a beat. First, a breath. Maybe even five seconds of silence, even if it felt like an eternity.

Then I'd ask:

"Alright - how far out is it? And what can we move around while we wait?"

Instead of turning the mistake into a personal attack, I'd try to make it a collaborative fix. Because here's the thing no one tells you: most mistakes on set aren't personal. They're situational. Time, pressure, lack of sleep - everyone's juggling it. If someone screws up, chances are they already feel like shit about it. Yelling just pushes them further down the hole. Everyone is in the same boat as you. Look at it from a macroscopic view, and you'll have a more informed outlook.

And trust me, people remember how you make them feel way longer than they remember what you shot.

Also, today, I keep contingency in my back pocket. Backup plans. I'd have another PA on standby or arrange for a separate Uber for gear if possible. Even a 15-minute delay buffer in the call sheet.

Because losing your rag usually comes from poor prep or poor perspective. Neither of which is worth blowing up your reputation over. Be prepared in advance, and you won't have that problem.

If that moment with Harry happened now, I'd treat it as a pressure test of leadership, not a personal insult to my competence. I'd use it to bring the team closer, not drive a wedge between us.

And who knows? If I'd done that back then, maybe I'd have been the one Harry called when that indie feature came around. Maybe he'd say, "Krish? Yeah, he kept things cool even when shit hit the fan. He's solid."

That's the version of me I work towards now.

Because if you want to keep climbing in this industry, you can't just know how to make a film - you've got to know how to keep people coming back to make one with you.

## Step 3: Hone Persuasion

This one's the most important, and I can say without boasting this is why I feel I can be a great producer. I rarely ever feel compelled to persuade someone.

Persuasion is your superpower - convincing investors, crews, or studios to back your vision. It's not sleazy; it's clear reasoning. Read books - The 48 Laws of Power by Robert Greene and How to Win Friends and Influence People by Dale Carnegie.

Start with small stakes: pitch a mate to try a new pub (£5 pint). Write three points - vibe, drinks, location - and practice in two minutes. Building confidence takes a day.

Scale up: join a free film group on Reddit's r/Filmmakers. Pitch a short film idea - £20,000 budget, thriller - to get crew feedback. Post: "Why would you join this?" Takes an hour, hones your sell. Study "Pitch Anything" by Oren Klaff - read its 50-page pitch framework in a weekend. Apply it on a real gig: volunteer for an indie via ProductionHive (free).

Convince a director to tweak a schedule - say, "Shooting earlier saves £200." One shoot day tests your sway. You need to test the waters, see what works, and learn why it works. Don't be a dick;

make others see what you see from your perspective and make them believe that you won't let them down. You need to have a vision that people can trust in; you're a leader, be a leader.

Persuasion, when it's done right, doesn't feel like pressure. It feels like a possibility.

I remember a time back in film school when we were prepping for our final short. We needed a small shop location for one of the key scenes, something authentic, something real. We found the perfect one: a little corner shop in West London with faded signage and shelves stacked high with crisps and instant noodles. Total visual gold.

The only problem? The owner, an older gentleman who'd run it for years, wasn't having it. At all. He didn't want cameras. Didn't want disruption. Didn't want the hassle. He barely let us finish the sentence before shaking his head.

Now, the younger me could've walked away. Said, "Okay, thanks for your time," and started looking for Plan B. But something told me there was a way in.

So I tried something different. I didn't start with "We need this." I asked him about his story away from the pressure of using his shop. Turns out he'd been running that shop for 27 years after coming from India. Yes, he was from the same city as me, so we found common ground. It was his father's before that. It had been through recessions, floods, and even a robbery or two. I listened, really listened, and when he was done, I said something like, "Honestly, that's exactly the kind of story we want our film to reflect. We want to show that kind of resilience. That's why your shop felt right."

Then came the offer: "We'll keep the crew small. We'll shoot early in the morning before customers come in. And here's the thing: we'll put your shop's real name in the film. Free promotion. Local pride. You'll be in the credits, too."

His whole posture changed. It wasn't a deal anymore; it was legacy and an offer from a newly made friend. And by the end of the chat, he was not only permitting us; he was telling us what angles would make the shop look "more alive." We even shot him in a cameo, stocking shelves in the background.

That was the moment I realised that persuasion isn't about being slick. It's about connection. It's about showing people how your vision helps their vision, even if they don't know they have one yet.

It's why I love being a producer. I don't have to manipulate. I just have to make people feel safe enough to dream with me.

You can practice this, too. Try to get your mate to try a new pub, seriously. Sell it like it's a mission. Build that pitch: 3 talking points, 2 minutes max. Then scale up. Use Reddit, or ProductionHive, or even strangers on the Tube. What you're doing isn't "selling" in the greasy sense; you're inviting people into your world. And if your world's worth entering, they'll come.

I've read "The 48 Laws of Power", "How to Win Friends and Influence People," and "Pitch Anything," and yeah, they help. But nothing teaches you like standing in front of a stubborn shopkeeper and convincing him to be part of something bigger than a transaction.

That's when you realise that persuasion isn't about getting what you want; It's about helping someone else see that they want it too.

## Step 4: Communicate Effectively

Talking right is non-negotiable - clear, concise, no waffle.

I've been on too many sets where simple communication is misunderstood. There are so many ways to interpret simple communication, and the least you could do is mitigate any room for confusion. Be clear and absolutely precise, and more importantly, ensure that the other person is on the same page as you.

Misunderstandings cost time and cash. Test it in film: join a student shoot. As a PA, relay one instruction, "Camera needs a new battery by 2 p.m.." and confirm it's done. It might sound easy, but this one simple situation can be misread in a hundred ways. For example, what battery, and where do they want it? How many do they want? It is a small example, but small things like this can compound operational inefficiencies. Getting a battery simple enough, right?

Wrong.

2 p.m. came and went. No battery. The camera died mid-take. We lost thirty minutes of sunlight, one scene had to be rewritten. When I asked what happened, the runner said, "You didn't say where to get it or what type." He'd assumed someone else was handling it, and by the time he checked in, the gear room was locked, and the AC had gone for lunch.

That small sentence, vague and unconfirmed, cost us two hours of reshuffling and about £300 in crew overtime. All because I thought I was being clear.

Since then, I've learned the power of precision. Now, I say: "We need the Alexa battery, fully charged, picked up from the gear van, and handed to the camera by 1:45 p.m. latest. Can you repeat that back to me?" Every time, I wait for them to confirm. I don't trust them, not because it's my job to make sure they know exactly what to do.

Miscommunication is like slow poison on set. It doesn't blow up instantly; it creeps in, erodes efficiency, builds frustration, and burns time. That's a luxury we don't have in filmmaking.

Since that East London mess, I've studied communication like it's a craft.

Read "Never Split the Difference" by Chris Voss - it's 30-page listening section (one evening) that teaches how to read people. Use it on set: ask a gaffer, "What's blocking you?" and rephrase their answer to check you got it. Find events on Eventbrite - free Q&As with UK filmmakers. Ask a producer, "How do you brief a crew fast?" Takes an evening; their tip is like numbered lists - sticks.

## Step 5: Put It All Together

Now combine them - patience, cool head, persuasion, clear talk - in a real project.

Produce a 3-minute short film, £200 budget. Use Google Docs (free) to plan: £100 for food/props, £100 for gear rental (borrow a mate's camera if skint). Recruit five crew via Meetupsell them on the project's vibe in a 100-word post (persuasion). Schedule one shoot day; when delays hit (patience), don't snap (cool head), suggest fixes, like cutting a scene. Brief everyone clearly: "We shoot scene one at 10 a.m., 30 minutes." Takes two weeks to prep, one day to shoot, and one week to edit (DaVinci Resolve, free). Screen it at a free local open mic search "film night [city]." Ask viewers, "Was it smooth?" Feedback shows your producer chops. Costs £200 max, takes a month, and proves you've got the personality to run a film.

**Why This Works**

In 2025's UK industry, 181 TV shows, £2.1 billion in films, as per BFI these traits are gold. Patience and calm keep you sane when shoots derail, persuasion lands funding in a market where indies risk collapse, per Screen International, and clear communication saves hours on chaotic sets. This plan's cheap (£32-£370), fast (six weeks), and practical free platforms, real sets, and small projects. You'll handle a £200 film, brief crews, and pitch ideas, ready for bigger gigs or to pivot if producing's not you. Start here, and you're not just a dreameryou're a producer who gets it done.

After writing almost every day, I got a chance to direct my own short film, "Cover of a Book," which I can say was the first film that felt like my style.

" The Cover of a Book" wasn't my first film technically, but it was the first one that felt like it came from my core. Before this, most of my work was tied to someone else's vision. Course assignments. Collaborations where I didn't have full creative control. Shoots where I was just happy to be on set, figuring out how to keep things afloat. But this one - this one was mine.

The idea came to me quietly, in a way most of my best ideas tend to. It didn't start with a script or a perfectly structured treatment. It started with a feeling. I couldn't describe it at the time - it was more like a mood. A kind of soft sadness. A weight. I wanted to make something intimate. Something that felt like you were flipping through the pages of a memory you didn't know you had.

Strangely, the first thing I turned to wasn't my camera - it was music.

I knew early on that I wanted the film to be structured around a song, not just accompanied by one. So I reached out to a singer whose voice felt like the kind of emotion I was chasing. Raw, honest, unfiltered. We sat down together with a composer, and we didn't just make a track - we built a world in sound. Every lyric, every note had to mean something. We weren't writing a song and slapping visuals on it. We were constructing a film that lived inside the music. I wanted my character to speak his emotions, not through words but through the music.

That was my first big moment - realising that storytelling doesn't have to start with a screenplay. It can start with a hum. A beat. An emotion that you stretch into form. That collaboration taught me how deeply music and story are tied. It also taught me to let go of control and trust collaborators who bring something I don't. The singer brought vulnerability. The composer brought soul. Together, they gave the story its heartbeat. We spent countless hours in the recording studio at MetFilm, finessing the rhythm, the tune, the words. We recorded instruments that have never been blended together. The song was about a friend grieving the death of his best friend.

We shot during the dead of winter in London. And not the cinematic kind of winter - I'm talking numb toes, frozen breath, and camera batteries dying mid-take. The kind of cold that tests your patience and your gear. I remember wrapping my scarf around my hands between takes just to keep feeling in my fingers. But somehow, in that brutal weather, we were trying to create warmth. That was the irony - freezing outside but trying to craft something tender onscreen.

I had so much on my plate. I was co-producing it, managing logistics, pulling favours from people I'd worked with on other gigs. Trying to keep the energy up on set while also keeping track of shot lists, continuity, and vibes. I was exhausted but also weirdly fuelled by adrenaline. I think I hadn't fully grasped yet that I was directing my film. Like, this wasn't just another job - this was my name, my vision, my gut on the line.

I hired my first professional actress for Cover of a Book - someone who'd actually done proper films, understood craft, and took the role seriously. And let me tell you, that changed everything.

Professionals bring a level of subtlety that you can't fake. She brought nuance, silence, stillness - stuff I didn't even write but instinctively felt was right. I remember watching her through the monitor and thinking, Damn. It is what it feels like when performance hits truth.

I didn't have to micromanage. I just had to guide. And that taught me a big lesson - directing isn't always about having the answers. Sometimes, it's just about creating space for the right things to happen.

Her presence grounded the whole film. It also raised the bar for me. I couldn't just coast. I had to match her energy with my own clarity of vision.

After every shooting day, I spent time collating my thoughts in my notebook, writing out what I learnt and how to improve.

The Cover of a Book was the first time I truly shot something that reflected my style - not what I thought a short film should look like, but what I wanted it to look like. There was more silence. More restraint. More emphasis on atmosphere than exposition. I leaned into natural light, reflective surfaces, and close-ups that lingered a bit too long. I wasn't chasing spectacle. I was chasing emotion.

I also started trusting my eyes more. Instead of asking, "Does this look good?" I started asking, "Does this feel right?" That shift changed everything.

There were plenty of mistakes. I overthought some scenes and underplanned others. Some takes didn't land. Time ran out. Shots had to be cut. But I stopped beating myself up for not having it all figured out. Because the magic of this film was in the process - the making of it taught me more than any textbook or tutorial ever could.

The Cover of a Book became my turning point. Not because it won any awards or blew up online (it didn't), but because it was the first time I could watch my own film and say, That feels like me. It was the beginning of me shaping a voice. A style. A way of working.

More than anything, it taught me how powerful it is to trust your instincts, even when you're not sure where they're leading you. Because that's what directing is, at the end of the day. Controlled chaos. Inspired guessing. Finding gold in the moments you didn't plan for.

This short film gave me a glimpse of the kind of stories I want to tell and how I want to tell them. Quiet, emotional, layered. Films that move slowly but hit deep. Looking back, I think this was the first time I felt like a real filmmaker.

Next up was my graduation film, a proof-of-concept short I produced, a step up from The Grandmaster's madness. The idea hit me late one night, scribbling in my notebook under a flickering bulb: an Indian boy duped into coming to the UK, promised a dream job, only to end up a slave. Heavy stuff, but I wanted to tell it- real, raw, with a punch that'd linger. MetFilm gave us a studio for the shoot, a rare treat, but when I walked in, my heart sank- four purple walls, a concrete floor, and nothing else. How do you make an Indian village out of this? Back home, a village is dust, huts, and cows wandering. Here, I had a blank slate and a budget tighter than a stingy uncle's wallet. But production's about solving, not sulking, so I rolled up my sleeves.

First, the ground villages need earth, not concrete. I found a builders' yard online, haggled 300 kilos of sand down to £ 50 delivered in sacks, I hauled into the studio myself, one back-breaking trip at a time. The delivery guy dumped them at the curb, smirking, "Good luck, mate." I dragged them in, sack by sack, sweat dripping, feeling every kilo in my spine. Spreading it out took hours - sand in my shoes, my hair, my lungs - but I felt like a kid building a fort, except this fort had to hold a story.

Next, the walls - purple wouldn't cut it. I hit up a DIY shop, bought 100 meters of brick-patterned wallpaper- cheap stuff, £30 total- and pasted it up with a mate from class, a lanky guy named Tom, who cursed every bubble. It looked flat, too fake, so we grabbed brown spray paint, £5 a can, and went wild- smudges, streaks, a bit of chaos. The smell was awful like a paint factory exploded, my hands stained brown for days, but step back, and it worked - an Indian village, rough and real, born from purple nothing.

The shoot was brutal, but I had a team that knew exactly what the vision was. I knew crew who were good at their roles, and I trusted them. I leaned on every runner trick I'd learned: angles over cash, hustle over kit.

That film was my bridge-student chaos to pro-stakes. Fast forward to after graduation, and I'm on Lucifer 2, my first cinema release as a production coordinator.

It wasn't short- it was a Malayalam feature with a big budget and bigger expectations, released on March 27, 2025, and now the most successful Malayalam film ever. I'd leveled up from runner to coordinator, wrangling a crew ten times the Grandmaster's size- hundreds of people, not 24. The Line producer hired me off a recommendation from a MetFilm gig where I'd kept a shoot alive through a power cut. My job? Keep the machine running schedules, locations, egos, and a dozen call sheets fluttering in my hands. No cooking this time- proper caterers with steel trays of biryani, thank God- but the pressure was insane. For me, no pressure at all because this time, if I had a problem, I could solve it with money, not just effort. I believe producing a no-budget film will teach you more about the fundamentals of production than a big-budget film ever will.

Lucifer 2 was a beast, but it paid off- cinema screens lit up, houses packed, my name in the credits, people actually saw, not just classmates.

Between The Grandmaster, the graduation film, and this, I'd learned the ropes: low-budget chaos builds you, gritty shorts sharpen you, and big-budget chaos tests you. Runner days still echoed cable I'd taped in Camden, every coffee I'd fetched in Hackney, every sandbag I'd hauled in Brixton led here. I'd gone from a newbie tripping over cables to a guy who could keep a blockbuster humming.

## How to get work in Production

I dabbled in my first few gigs in London in Chapter 1. I didn't go in-depth to explain what went into actually making those connections to get on set and how to progress in the right direction.

Starting in the film industry can feel like a labyrinth, exciting yet daunting, chaotic yet full of opportunity. For someone fresh out of film school or just starting out, securing that first gig, especially as a runner, is often the hardest but the most crucial step.

The experience you gain from working as a runner on set opens doors and builds a foundation for everything else in your career. You get to observe how productions work behind the scenes, learn the rhythm of the crew, and establish the relationships that will take you further in the industry.

So, how do you land your first gig? For me, it wasn't about waiting for the perfect opportunity to fall into my lap. It was about going out and finding it. Here's how I did it and how you can, too.

## The Hustle: Going the Extra Mile

I started writing this book to understand this maze of an industry. The metrics and the people who were in it just didn't match up. When I first decided I wanted to break into film production, the one thing I realized quickly was that nobody was going to hand me a job. The industry doesn't care about your aspirations; it cares about what you can contribute right now. So, I had to find a way to stand out. A massive part of this was sheer persistence.

I knew I needed to make an impact, and I needed to do it in a way that others wouldn't. I started with the basics: a solid CV. A clean, no-nonsense resume that showcased my passion, my ambition, and my willingness to learn. But the next step, getting it in front of the right people, that's where things got real.

I spent a couple of weeks dropping off my CV in person at production companies, studios, and post-production houses in Soho. There was something very direct and human about walking into these places and handing over my CV. It wasn't about handing over a piece of paper; it was about making a real connection. I remember being nervous at first, unsure if I was wasting my time. But every time I walked into a new company, it was another chance to introduce myself to stand out from the flood of digital applications.

Soho was a busy, bustling area full of film professionals, but there was something about seeing the faces of the people behind the names in the email inbox. Getting lost in the sea of emails and LinkedIn messages was too easy. The in-person approach allowed me to get a read on the vibe of the company and the people who worked there. It let me make an impression that an email just couldn't.

Personal connections are gold; 70% of jobs in creative industries come from networks, as per Creative Access Opportunities. Your persistence, applying 300+ times, aligns with industry norms where it takes 2-3 years to land a paid role, per Prospects.ac.uk Film

Industry Jobs. It's not just about CVs; it's about showing up, which your in-person hustle did.

## Challenges for Newcomers

The film industry is notoriously competitive for entry-level positions, with platforms like My First Job in Film indicating that a single job posting for a production runner can attract over 200 applications in 2024 My First Job in Film. This high rejection rate underscores the need for persistence. Additionally, ScreenSkills reports that 88% of UK film industry workers are freelancers, meaning securing a steady role requires skill and a network of contacts who can vouch for you. Your proactive approach helps build this network early on, aligning with the industry's freelance nature and the need for constant outreach.

Once I had made the rounds in Soho, I expanded my search to Shoreditch, a hub for creatives and indie film production companies.

I quickly learned that the environment in Shoreditch was different from Soho. Here, I was walking into smaller, more experimental companies where personal connections mattered even more. But while the vibe was different, the principles were the same.

## The Importance of Location

Soho and Shoreditch are epicenters of film production in London, with Soho alone hosting over 1,000 production-related businesses, as per Film London in 2024. By targeting these areas, you positioned yourself in the heart of the industry, where opportunities are more likely to arise.

The BFI notes a 15% increase in production activity outside London since 2020, but for newcomers, London's concentration of companies makes it the ideal starting point for BFI.

The key was to be relentless. I wasn't just handing out CVs; I was showing up and letting people know I was serious. If they weren't hiring at that moment, I'd follow up, show gratitude for their time, and keep the door open for future opportunities.

## Persistence Pays Off

Creative Access's 2024 survey found that 60% of entry-level film professionals secured their first job through repeated outreach and follow-ups rather than a single application, as per Creative Access Opportunities. Prospects.ac.uk also states that, on average, it takes aspiring filmmakers 2-3 years to secure their first paid role, often starting with unpaid or low-paid positions.

# LinkedIn: Connecting with a Purpose

One of the tools in building my network was LinkedIn. But simply connecting with people wasn't enough. I needed to engage with the right people, not just anyone. I started a routine of messaging people in production companies every single day. And when I say every day, I mean every day. It was time-consuming, but it worked. I wasn't just sending generic messages; I was tailoring each message to the specific person I was reaching out to. I did my research: I'd find someone at a company who seemed to be working in a role that aligned with my goals, whether it was a producer, a production coordinator, or even another runner.

I remember one particular conversation that stuck with me. I messaged a production coordinator at a mid-size company in London. The message was short but direct. I introduced myself, mentioned my relevant experience, and expressed a genuine interest in learning more about the company. I didn't beg for a job; I simply showed I was eager to connect. Within a few hours, they replied. It wasn't an offer of a job, but they did offer a recommendation for another contact at a different company. That single message led to a series of introductions, and within weeks, I had secured a couple of interviews for runner positions. The lesson here is simple: don't just aim for a job; aim to build a relationship.

## Building Meaningful Connections

I can't stress enough how important building meaningful, authentic relationships is in this industry. It's not just about who you know but about who knows you and, more importantly, who remembers you. This can't be achieved through transactional, "what's in it for me" relationships. It's about giving as much as you take.

While searching for a runner gig, I began to see the value in connecting with people, not just for immediate gain, but for the future. A lot of people in the industry are always looking for talent, whether it's for a film shoot coming up in two weeks or a bigger project they have in the works. The more I networked and built rapport, the more I realized how often I would be recommended for roles simply because I had made an effort to connect with people on a deeper level. Sometimes, this meant offering my help for free on smaller projects simply because I knew the person needed it. It wasn't about getting paid. It was about proving I was reliable and easy to work with.

One key lesson I learned was to always follow up. If someone gave me advice or pointed me in the right direction, I would send a simple thank you message. Later, when I had secured a position, I would update them on my progress. That way, they would know I was serious about growing my career and would be more likely to think of me when new opportunities came up.

## Film Festivals and Events: The Best Networking Grounds

I also realized that film festivals and industry events were incredible opportunities to meet the people I wanted to work with. While these events can seem overwhelming at first, with so many people milling around, trying to make their own connections, they're some of the best places to make lasting, meaningful relationships. It's one thing to meet someone at a networking event and add them on LinkedIn, but it's entirely different when you meet them in person, exchange a few ideas, and build rapport over a drink or during a panel discussion.

I vividly remember attending the London Film Festival one year. I didn't have a project at the festival but knew it was a great place to meet other aspiring filmmakers and industry professionals. I walked into a session on production logistics and found myself chatting with a producer who worked on a well-known indie feature. We talked about everything from the challenges of coordinating a shoot to the latest films we had both seen. It wasn't about pitching myself for a job. It was just a conversation. A few months later, that same producer gave me an opportunity to work as a runner on a mid-sized film project.

Film festivals aren't just for filmmakers showing off their work; they're an ideal space for learning and networking. Whether it's a talk, a panel, or a simple coffee break, it's the perfect environment to meet people who might be looking for exactly what you offer.

## Making Sense of the Chaos: Staying Persistent

The road to landing your first gig is a long one, and it's full of chaos. There will be rejections, missed opportunities, and frustrations. I can't tell you how many times I thought I was close to landing a job, only to hear nothing back. But in retrospect, I realize that persistence is key. And, just as important, the ability to stay calm in the chaos.

When I first started, I could feel the pressure building the anxiety of finding my first paid gig, the frustration of waiting for callbacks, and the constant hustle. But over time, I learned how to manage that stress. I understood that this wasn't a sprint; it was a marathon. Every no was just one step closer to a yes.

As much as the grind can feel like chaos, it's also a reminder that every step you take is leading somewhere. The key is staying focused, putting in the hours, and building relationships that will pay off. Whether it's a cold email, a LinkedIn message, or a casual conversation at a film festival, every interaction is an opportunity to make a lasting connection.

# Conclusion: Persistence, Strategy, and Meaningful Connections

Landing your first gig in production as a runner isn't easy. It's about persistence, strategy, and the ability to make meaningful connections. Whether you're dropping off CVs in Soho or attending a film festival, every action you take should be part of a larger, longer-term plan. Film production is a collaborative business, and the connections you build early on will determine your career trajectory.

You'll eventually find that first gig by putting yourself out there, staying patient, and showing that you're willing to go the extra mile. And once you do, you'll realize that getting the job is only the beginning, the real work is in proving yourself as reliable, capable, and someone people want to work with. So, take a deep breath, stay persistent, and trust the process. The industry may be chaotic, but with the right mindset, you can navigate it and find your way in.

# Chapter 3 - Riding the Waves – Employment Shifts in the UK Film Industry

The film industry's a beast, and London's its beating heart - wild, unpredictable, full of traps and payoffs. I started this book to make sense of it, to crack open the numbers and the people running the show, because trust me, they don't always line up.

This chapter sets you up for what's coming: a hard look at the UK film scene from 2020 to 2025, a five-year sprint of crashes, booms, and comebacks.

It's not just stats or headlines - it's the ground truth of what it takes to break through, from knowing who's hiring to dodging the industry's curveballs. If you're eager to get started, this is your first step toward understanding the game.

When I landed in London, I had no contacts, no insider tricks, just a need to make films. The industry didn't care about my dreams; it wanted skills, hustle, and proof I could deliver. That's the deal here: nobody hands you a gig. You've got to show up, stand out, and keep pushing, whether you're aiming to direct, produce, or just get your foot in the door.

What follows in this chapter is the full picture - how the UK's film world ticked over half a decade, with billions spent, jobs created, and egos bruised. It's a map of the chaos: studios pumping out blockbusters, indies scraping by, TV shows stealing the spotlight, all while the world threw punches like pandemics and strikes.

I spent years talking to people and attempting to understand how the numbers align with reality so that we can accurately manage our expectations based on facts rather than feelings.

I'm not here to bore you with spreadsheets but to show what those numbers mean for someone starting out, trying to turn their passion into a paycheck.

The UK's film industry isn't just one thing - it's a split screen. On one side, you've got massive sets in Pinewood or Shepperton, where Hollywood's splashing cash on superhero flicks or fantasy epics. On the other, small crews in Hackney warehouses, betting everything on a script, nobody's heard of.

In 2025, London's a global player, but it's not LA or Mumbai - it's got its own rhythm, its own rules. This chapter breaks it down: how money flows, who's getting hired, and where the jobs hide. You'll see the gaps - between what the industry says and what it does, between the glossy premieres and the freelancers eating noodles to make rent. My story's in there too - not as a hero, but as someone who learned the hard way, starting at the bottom and fighting for every chance.

Why does this matter? Because if you're reading this, you're probably like I was: fired up but clueless, wondering how to crack this world open. The pages ahead give you the raw data: production budgets, job markets, and global standings, all tied to what it's like on the ground.

It's not just about the UK either; I'll stack it up against other hubs and show you where London fits. But more than that, it's about surviving the hustle. I've got tips, not from a textbook, but from grinding it out and learning what works when you've no name and no budget.

This chapter is your crash course, packed with numbers that tell the industry's story - spending trends, crew demands, box office swings - without losing the human side. You'll get a sense of what's possible, what's brutal, and how to navigate both. It's for anyone who's ever watched a film and thought, "I want to make that happen." Directors, producers, runners, it doesn't matter - you need to know the machine you're stepping into.

## The industry from 2020 to 2025

From 2020 to 2025, employment here's been a rollercoaster - COVID smashing it flat, booms lifting it sky-high, strikes shaking it like a rickety bridge. I've dug deep into the numbers - BFI stats, Bectu surveys, ScreenSkills forecasts, whatever I could scrape off the web - to map this chaos. It isn't just cold data; it's a survival guide that I have compiled over the years. So, grab a steaming chai, settle into your charpai - or whatever passes for one in your London flat - and let's unpack this tale of those years, what they mean for the future, and how we ride these waves without drowning.

Understanding the film industry as a business helps us forecast how we can position ourselves as creatives to withstand periods when work is at its lowest. The film industry in the UK isn't the biggest in the world and you have every right to question why I left one of the biggest film industries in the world to struggle to find work in the UK, but that's a whole other story.

To understand where the UK stands, I did a study on its position against the world's biggest industries - Hollywood, Bollywood and Chinese-language cinema.

The film industry's a global game, and the UK's a serious player, but it's not the biggest. By 2025, it's set to employ 140,000-145,000 people - decent, but dwarfed by the US at 2.6 million jobs and India topping 6 million.

Yet, the UK's output tells a different story: £5.6 billion spent on production in 2024, with a sharp focus on high-end TV (HETV).

That's not just numbers - it's a signal of where the work is, what's valued, and how a small island holds its own against giants. Let's unpack this for anyone looking to break in so you know what you're stepping into and where you can carve a spot.

Starting with jobs. The UK's 140,000-145,000 employment by 2025, projected by ScreenSkills, cover everything - directors, grips, editors, runners. It's a tight ecosystem compared to the US, where 2.6 million jobs, per the Motion Picture Association, span Hollywood's blockbusters to regional ads. India's over 6 million, driven by Bollywood and regional cinemas like Tamil and Telugu, per FICCI reports, is a giant fueled by sheer volume - 2,000 films a year versus the UK's 191 in 2024. This difference is massive.

The UK's smaller pool means competition's fierce: a runner gig can get 200 applications, says My First Job in Film. But it's also focused - jobs cluster in London, Manchester, or studios like Pinewood, so you're not chasing ghosts across a continent. For newbies, this means targeting hubs like Soho or Leavesden, where roles from PA to VFX artists are concentrated, and persistence lands work faster than in sprawling markets.

Now, let's talk about spending. The UK's £5.6 billion in 2024, per BFI, split £2.1 billion on films and £3.4 billion on HETV - think House of the Dragon or The Crown. That's massive for a country of 67 million, outpacing per-capita spending in larger economies. The

US, with $30 billion annually, leans on Marvel-sized budgets, while India's $2.5 billion supports thousands of low-cost films.

The UK's edge is efficiency: tax credits (40% for indies under £15 million) and skilled crews stretch every pound. HETV's the star - 181 shows in 2024 versus 191 films - driving jobs for sound mixers, ADs, and even caterers. For you, this screams opportunity: HETV's hunger means more entry-level gigs (runners, PAs) than cinema, especially on streaming sets for Netflix or Amazon. Check Mandy.com - HETV posts outnumber film 3-to-1, paying £100-£150/day for starters.

Why does the UK punch above its weight? Focus and reputation. Unlike the US's scattered indie scene or India's regional sprawl, the UK bets big on quality - films like All of Us Strangers or shows like Succession win global eyes. HETV's growth, up 31% from the strike-hit slump of 2023, according to BFI, draws Hollywood to Shepperton, with 25 streaming films adding £511 million. This isn't volume - it's precision. Crews here are world-class, trained via ScreenSkills for 21,000 new jobs by 2026.

For aspiring producers or directors, it's a goldmine: smaller teams mean you learn fast, maybe jumping from PA to 3rd AD in a year. But it's brutal too - 88% of workers freelance, per ScreenSkills, so you're hustling between gigs, building contacts to stay booked.

Globally, the UK is a middleweight with heavyweight clout. The US dominates in scale, with a $11 billion box office, compared to the UK's £979 million, but lacks the UK's HETV pipeline.

India churns out films but struggles with infrastructure; only 10% match the UK's polish.

For you, this means the UK's sweet spot: enough jobs to start (145,000), enough funding (£5.6 billion) to support bold projects, and a reputation that opens doors abroad. Want in? Hit London's job boards, network at free BFI events, and aim for HETV - it's where the industry's betting big and where you can grow from nobody to somebody. The evidence suggests that the UK is a middleweight champion, relying heavily on US investment (86% inward), while India and China dominate their domestic markets; France and Japan are smaller peers.

## Global Influence and Cultural Impact

The UK's cultural clout - Harry Potter, Bond, Oppenheimer nabs 10.5% of top 200 films' £13.4 billion (2012-2021, CRESCINE), with 23 Oscars/BAFTAs in 2021/22. Hollywood's $42 billion share (2019 peak) and India's 80%+ domestic dominance (Bollywood rules South Asia) overshadow, but the UK's niche is prestige.

## Unexpected Detail: Tax Incentives

The UK's 40% tax relief for indies under £15 million (GOV.UK, 2025) and 29.25% VFX rebates lure blockbusters like Snow White, unlike India's low-cost chaos or US's $750 million California credits (Entertainment Partners, 2025), giving it a global edge in attracting inward investment (86%, BFI 2024).

## Unexpected Detail: Studio Space Edge

By 2025, Greater London's studio space edges LA's, with Pinewood and Shepperton pulling Snow White. Unlike India's Mumbai chaos or the US's sprawl, the UK shines in this niche, with a land of more craft.

## Findings:

The Numbers Paint a Picture of Chaos and Comebacks. Let's rewind to 2020, the year the world hit pause and the UK film industry took a thrashing that'd make a Baahubali villain wince. Social Films pegs employment at 86,000 jobs, a significant decline from the more robust days of 2019, with 75% in production and distribution and the rest in exhibition cinemas, festivals, and screenings. That's a drop of 28,000 jobs, representing a 24.6% decline from an estimated 114,000, all thanks to COVID-19 turning sets into ghost towns. The BFI's clock production spend was £2.84 billion, a 21% plunge from £3.6 billion the year before lockdowns left cameras dusty, lights off, and crews twiddling their thumbs or queuing for benefits. Cinemas sat empty, popcorn machines cold, while freelancers, the gig's lifeblood, scraped by on furlough if lucky, prayers if not.

Fast forward to 2021, hope crept in like a monsoon breeze after a scorching drought. Statista marks jobs at 106,000, a 23% leap from '20's gloom, as production spending doubled to £5.64 billion. Tax reliefs and a backlog of shelved scripts kicked things into gear. Sound stages hummed, runners dashed with lukewarm teas, and DOPs barked through the clatter. It was a proper comeback, a hero rising from the ashes, Bollywood-style.

Then 2022, the industry roared like a lion. BFI reports £6.27 billion in spending, up 37% from '21£1.97 billion on films, £4.3 billion on glossy HETV for your sofa. Jobs? No hard number, but I'd eyeball 120,000-125,000, riding that cash wave.

## Graph Placeholder 1: Employment Boom (2020-2022)

Description: Line graph, x-axis years (2020-2022), y-axis jobs (thousands). Starts at $86,000 in 2020, climbs to $106,000 in 2021, and peaks at approximately $125,000 in 2022, with a slight curve. Overlay a dotted spending line at £2.84 billion, £5.64 billion, and £6.27 billion, mirroring the rise. Label it "The Boom Begins," with an arrow at '22: "I Land Here!" Gold for spend, green for jobs, Diwali sparkler vibes.

But 2023? A jolt like a rickshaw hitting a pothole. US strikes - Writers Guild, SAG-AFTRA sent shockwaves, crashing film spending 31% to £1.36 billion from £2.2 billion (BFI), dragging total spending to £4.23 billion.

Bectu's February '24 survey reveals 68% of 4,000+ workers are jobless, 30% are idle for three months, 58% are hopeless, 88% are fretting about rent, and 75% are battling mental health issues. I felt its gigs vanish, Camden cables one day, radiator hum the next. A large number of my industry friends took the sharp end of this sword and had to change career paths or head back home to pursue film. This was bleak.

Cue 2024, the hero dusted off his kurta.

Variety shouts £5.6 billion. £2.2 billion film, £3.4 billion HETV. a 31% leap from '23's ashes. Jobs bounced back to around 120,000, with HETV reeling in cash from Netflix, Amazon, and the BBC. Co-productions shrank 29 vs. 48 in '22 hinting at a UK-focused game.

Then, on April 8th, 2025, at midnight BST, the clock ticks over. ScreenSkills calls for 21,000 more crew - 15,130 to 20,770 to match £7.66 billion spent, and studios are booked solid. Bectu pushes for freelancer aid, and I'd bet jobs hit 140,000-145,000 by year-end, based on a gut feeling of an upward trend. With Lucifer 2's wrapping up, my name was on the screens from London to Kerala.

## Graph Placeholder 2: Employment Rollercoaster (2023-2025)

Description: Line graph, x-axis years (2023-2025), y-axis jobs (thousands). Drops to ~90,000 in 2023 "Strike Slump" rises to ~120,000 in 2024, spikes to ~140,000 in 2025, starred "Now!" at April. Bar chart overlay: £4.23 billion, £5.6 billion, £7.66 billion, "Strikes to Surge." Grey dip, gold boom cricket match drama.

## The future of the film industry - Where do we see it going?

What's the UK's film hub got in store from 2025 on? It's not Hollywood's giant or Bollywood's sprawl, but with 140,000-145,000 jobs, £5.6 billion spent in 2024, and a laser focus on high-end TV (HETV), London punches hard for its size. Compared to the US's 2.6 million jobs or India's 6 million, it's leaner, but that's its strength - a tight, efficient, global approach. This chapter maps the next five years: more cash, new tech, job shifts, and what it means for you - whether you're eyeing director, producer, or runner.

**Jobs: Growth with a Catch**

By 2025, the UK's film industry employs 140,000-145,000, per ScreenSkills, with London hogging half-think 70,000 roles from gaffers to VFX coders.

By 2030, expect 160,000-170,000 jobs, driven by HETV and studio expansions. Film London predicts £9.5 billion in investment by 2029, adding 10,000 roles, such as camera operators and editors, particularly in hubs like Pinewood and Leavesden. The US, with 2.6 million jobs, spreads work more widely - from LA to Atlanta - but London's focus means faster starts. India's 6 million jobs lean low-budget; here, £100-£150/day runner gigs are standard.

The catch? Skills gaps. BFI flags 21,000 new workers needed by 2026, with coders, VR techs, and sustainability leads in demand. Training's lagging - £100 million needed yearly, says ScreenSkills, but only £60 million is funded. For you, this means an opportunity to join free BFI Future Film Festival workshops or ScreenSkills' Creative Skills Academy, which has trained 2,333 individuals since 2022. Learn Unreal Engine or green production - skills short now, gold by 2030. Without them, you're stuck competing for 200+ applications per PA role, per My First Job in Film. Talking about advancements in skills, we have to talk about AI and how that will shape jobs.

# AI's Grip on London's Film Future

Tech is reshaping London's skyline by 2030. AI's already cutting costs - editing software like Runway trims £10,000 off post-production. By 2028, expect AI scripting tools on 30% of HETV, predicts Screen Alliance, freeing writers for polish, not drafts. VR's bigger - Pinewood's virtual sets, used for Andor season 2 in 2025, save £50,000 on-location shoots. For directors, VR means pre-viz freedom; for runners, it's learning Unreal Engine or getting left behind. India is slow on VR, lacking studios, but the US leads with $500 million in virtual technology. London's catching up, with £750,000 from City Hall for tech training by 2027.

AI's not just a buzzword; it's rewriting how films get made in London, and by 2030, it'll shake up every set from Pinewood to Hackney. In 2025, the UK is pumping £5.6 billion into production, with 140,000-145,000 jobs, and AI is already slicing costs and sparking fights. For directors, producers, or runners, this isn't sci-fi - it's your next gig, your next skill, or your next headache.

Right now, AI's cutting grunt work. By 2028, Screen Alliance predicts that 30% of HETV shows - think Slow Horses season 6 - will utilize AI for scripting first drafts, freeing writers for polishing. It's fast: a 30-second trailer cut in hours, not days.

Producers save cash; 2025's Black Bag used AI for crowd VFX, slashing £20,000. But it's not all rosy - X posts from editors gripe about AI flooding jobs with cheap cuts, and Bectu flags 5% of post roles at risk by 2027.

For you, AI's a tool, not a boss. Learn it - ScreenSkills offers free AI webinars, teaching the basics, such as Adobe Firefly for VFX. Takes a weekend makes you a hire that studios want for Andor-style sets.

Runners, train in AI logging; it's £100/day work logging dailies.

1,000 new AI-skilled jobs will hit London by 2029, per Film London. AI's here, reshaping HETV and indies, and it's your shot to ride the wave or get left behind. The way I see it is parallel to the introduction of sound in film.

## Spending: Cash Keeps Flowing

London's £5.6 billion spend in 2024 - £2.1 billion for films, £3.4 billion for HETV - sets the pace. By 2030, Film London projects £7-8 billion, fueled by tax credits (40% for indies under £15 million) and streamers like Netflix and Amazon.

HETV's the engine - think Bridgerton Season 4 or Slow Horses Season 6, filming in 2025 with stars like Luke Thompson and Gary Oldman. Films won't slack either: 2025's Black Bag (Soderbergh, Fassbender) and Masters of the Universe (Idris Elba, Jared Leto) show London's pull for A-listers. Compared to the US's $30 billion or India's $2.5 billion, the UK's spend is precise - less waste, more polish. Every pound funds jobs: £200/day for grips, £500 for DPs.

Indies are the wildcard. According to Screen International, the new 40% tax credit could double the number of small films from 300 in 2030 to 600 in 2024 if equity financing increases. However, streamers dominate; for producers, this means pitching bold films, such as Last Swim's teen angst, shot across Camden and Hampstead.

## Reflection: Making Sense of the Madness

This five-year saga is a Bollywood blockbuster with villains, heroes, and twists galore. 2020's COVID slashed jobs like a dacoit through sugarcane; 86,000 stood, a shadow of what was before. '21 and '22 brought the hero's rise from £ 5.64 billion to £6.27 billion, with tax breaks and streaming giants flooding the fields.

'23's plot twist stung - US strikes washed gigs away, BFI's £1.36 billion drop was stark, Bectu's 68% jobless report a dagger. '24 flipped it - £5.6 billion, HETV at £3.4 billion. I'm on Lucifer 2, crew ten times The Grandmaster's size, cash flowing like the Ganges. '25's climax - £7.66 billion, 21,000-crew call booms big, but skills gaps and burnout loom.

My reel? Runner in '22, sandbags bruising, to Lucifer 2 in '25, Jugaad (Indian slang for getting something in a tricky but sustainable manner) built me, with scars and all.

The future is optimistic, with scope for more job opportunities, particularly in areas that require more skilled workers. The implementation of AI is inevitable, and learning how to use it to your advantage is key to your survival. Cash in film is steady, but HETV is mainly where most of the money is being pumped into.

What did your last five years look like?

## The Conundrum: Chasing Dreams Through Side Gigs

This industry is riddled with people who are forced to work a different job than what they really want to get into. This makes it extremely hard to keep track of where your career has headed and the progress you've made.

This hustle really plays in your conscience and can deter your progress drastically.

First off, let's talk about why this happens. Films are magic on screen but behind the scenes? It's a circus hierarchical, cutthroat, and packed with more egos than a Mumbai rush-hour train. The roles everyone wants - director, DP, writer - are locked behind gates guarded by experience, connections, and pure luck. Nobody starts there unless you're some nepotism kid with an uncle at Netflix. For the rest of us - like me, the path is through the grunt work. Runner, spark, production assistant - jobs that pay peanuts and feel light-years from your vision. I wanted to yell "action!" but ended up taping gels in Reading, praying I didn't knock over another stand. That's the deal: you take what you can get to stay in the room.

The problem? These side gigs aren't just stepping stones; they're quicksand. You're so busy running - literally, that you lose sight of where you're headed. Days blur into 14-hour shoots, nights into job apps or bar shifts to cover rent. I'd come home to my dorm, knackered, hands raw from cables, and think, "Am I closer to directing? Producing? Anything?"

It's like you're climbing a ladder, but the rungs keep vanishing. You're a spark today, a runner tomorrow, maybe a PA next week, and there's no clear line to "cinematographer" or whatever's burning in your chest.

Progress? Feels like a myth when you're too skint to buy a new SD card.

Let's get real about the mental toll. This conundrum is a mind-mangler.

You start doubting yourself - hard. I remember a low point in '23, sparking on a Shoreditch promo, taping cables while the DOP barked orders. I'm thinking, "This is it? Years dreaming, and I'm a glorified electrician?" Imposter syndrome creeps in - am I even good enough to make it? Everyone's hustling - runners eyeing my spark gig, sparks eyeing the gaffer's chair - and you're paranoid you're falling behind. Social media doesn't help; it makes it even more difficult. I can only speak for myself, but my social life is pretty non-existent. How can you have one if you're working 15-hour days? Even if you do get time, you'd rather get some sleep than socialise.

Comparison to other peers is a poison, too - a crew member you worked with before posts about their "indie short at Sundance," and you're like, "I'm still fetching lattes."

Keeping track of your career feels impossible when you're juggling survival jobs that don't scream "future filmmaker."

And the industry loves this trap - it thrives on it. Crews are freelance, gigs are short, and there's always someone hungrier waiting to take your spot. You say yes to everything, music videos, ads, that dodgy student film - because saying no might mean no calls tomorrow.

That's the conundrum's grip: you're stuck proving yourself in roles you don't want, hoping someone notices you're more than a pair of hands. Meanwhile, your actual goal feels like a mirage.

Money's another kick in the teeth. London's not cheap, rent's a killer, and entry-level film gigs pay like it's 1995. A runner's day rate might hit £100; sparks may be £200. Compare that to bar work, £12/hour, steady shifts, and it's tempting to ditch sets for a tap. I knew guys who'd PA by day, drive Deliveroo by night, and still couldn't afford a decent lens. Me? I'd stretch £80 from a Reading gig - chips on the train, praying my Oyster card didn't die. How do you track progress when you're broke, burning out, and your "career" feels like a patchwork of odd jobs?

You can't - it's chaos.

The worst part? The disconnect. You're on set, surrounded by the buzz - cameras rolling, lights humming - but you're not in it. You're the guy fetching batteries, not framing shots. I felt it on that Camden music video - rain spitting, gaffer raging, me taping cables while the director and DP sculpted magic. I was close but miles away. It's like spending hours buying ingredients to make a biryani, then giving it to someone else to make, and then you can't eat it.

You're there but not there, and it's tough to see how "runner today" becomes "DOP tomorrow."

But here's the flip side - not to get all sunny, but it's not all doom if you are smart and start looking at sets through a different lens.

Those side gigs, as much as they suck sometimes, teach you the game. Hauling gear in Hackney showed me how sets flow - cues, chaos, teamwork. Sparking taught me light - stuff I'd never learn from YouTube. I'd jot down notes in my dorm. Today, I learned about how to use flags; tomorrow, I'll watch the gaffer more closely. It's messy, but it's data, bhai.

You're building a map, even if it feels like scribbles. The trick is keeping one eye on those gigs and the other on your dream - tough when you're knackered, but that's the fight.

The industry's structure doesn't make it easier. Freelancing means no straight path -gigs zig-zag, and "progress" isn't a promotion but a better call sheet. I went from runner to spark to Lucifer 2 coordinator - not linear, more like a drunk autorickshaw ride. Tracking that? Most crew I met were the same - grips moonlighting as bartenders, PAs editing shorts at 2 a.m., all wondering, "Am I getting there?" No one knows - that's the conundrum's sting.

It's worse for outsiders like me—the desi kid in London, with no industry uncles to pull strings. You're fighting not just the grind but the gatekeepers. Again, I don't blame any of my shortcomings on being an outsider; everyone has their own difficulties.

You're stuck proving you're more than a runner, more than a spark, while the clock ticks and your mates back home post about "real" careers. Still, there's a weird beauty in it, bhai. Every crap job's a story. They stack up, not just as paychecks but as grit. I'd look back after a year. "Okay, I moved." Not clear, not pretty, but forward.

The conundrum forces you to hustle smarter - network in pubs, not LinkedIn; learn on set, not just in class. It's jugaad - making it work when the path's a mess. You track progress by feel - more confidence, better chats, a nod from a gaffer who yelled last week.

This grind's universal - every filmmaker's caught in it. That Camden gaffer? He wanted to direct, too, but bills don't wait. The Brixton runner? Writing scripts between coffee runs. We're all side-hustling toward the dream, dodging burnout, piecing together a career like a dodgy jigsaw. It's why I kept a notebook - scribbled wins, losses, and lessons. It wasn't a CV, just proof I wasn't standing still. You've gotta hold onto that, or the conundrum will swallow you whole. This life is hard to explain to people with a linear growth structure. You might sound crazy, but they don't know what you know. Keep going and believe in yourself; don't wait for someone to believe in you.

So yeah, it's a riddle work that you don't want to chase what you do, and good luck knowing if you're winning. The industry's built that way - it keeps the hungry scrambling, the dreamers tough.

# Chapter 4 -The Camera's Eye – Learning the Craft

My love for cameras started even before I ever came to London. I remember that I hated forgetting moments, and I wanted a way to capture them. I remember the day I got my first camera as if it were a slow-motion tracking shot from a coming-of-age indie film, minus the rain and orchestral score.

My dad, reluctantly but patiently, took me to Vijay Sales, that chaotic temple of tech in Mumbai, where everything is stacked, beeping, and on sale. If you've ever been to one, you know the vibe. Bright fluorescent lights, floor-to-ceiling displays of gadgets, and at least five different versions of every product, none of which the staff will let you touch unless you're already halfway through a purchase. The day was hot, and the store was packed with customers who couldn't resist the latest deals.

I had done all the research - YouTube videos, Reddit threads, random photography forums where everyone has a wildly different opinion on what a "starter" camera should be. I had my heart set on a Sony model that, frankly, was way out of my budget. Still, I hovered near it as it might magically drop in price if I stared long enough.

Then, this salesman walked up to me, wearing a sharp shirt and with too much gel in his hair, and asked what I was into. I said, "Filmmaking, photography... I want to start shooting."

He smiled, the kind of smile sales guys are trained to do. He asked me why I liked the Sony, and back then, I knew nothing about why it was a better choice than the starter cameras. Instead of upselling me some expensive kit, he paused and walked me over to another shelf. That's when I saw it: the Nikon D3400. Entry-level. Lightweight. Not flashy.

My dad raised an eyebrow at the price; it was still a big ask for someone who had no clue about the pricing of cameras. But the salesman threw in a basic strap and a flimsy black camera bag and called it a deal. That bag looked like it belonged to a courier guy, but to me, it was a badge of honor.

We walked out with the camera, no extended warranty, no tripod, no SD card even. Just that D3400, the strap, and a quietly bubbling obsession that would shape the next few years of my life. That D3400 came with me everywhere. At first, I just took photos around the house. My parents, the ceiling fan with motion blur, which I thought looked "cinematic." Back then, I didn't know that you could load off an SD card after it was full. So, I was extremely careful about what I shot. I treated it like a film camera. I was scared it would run out, and I would miss out on moments.

Any time we traveled - whether it was a family road trip or a proper getaway I'd bring the camera along like it was part of my body. My fingers used to wrap around the side of the camera like glue; it never ever fell off, no matter what I did. I used to run with it, dance with it on holidays, and even leave it hanging outside a moving car - I never dropped that camera even once.

At airports, I hated straps, so it was a little difficult going through security. On trains, I'd point it out the window, trying to track the movement of passing trees like I'd seen in Wes Anderson montages. Half the time, my batteries died before we even reached the hotel.

But still, I kept filming. It wasn't serious at first. I didn't storyboard or plan. I just felt my way through shots. A kid playing cricket on a beach. A temple bell swinging in slow motion. The way the sunlight filtered through palm leaves - stuff no one else in my family noticed but made me stop walking mid-conversation. They'd roll their eyes. I'd say, "Just one second, I need to get this." Spoiler: It was never one second.

And once I started editing those clips into little travel videos, I was hooked. I'd stay up late cutting footage, adding emotional royalty-free music, and incorporating cheesy text transitions like "LA, 2016" in cursive font. Looking back now, they were rough. Shaky, handheld pans, overexposed skies, completely off-white balance. But in those moments, I felt like I was capturing something bigger than just a trip; I was telling stories.

Each video was its own short film. No dialogue, no budget, and no real structure - just mood and memory stitched together. It felt like I was archiving not just where we went but who I was in that moment. That, to me, was more than enough. After using this camera for about a year on the auto setting, I ventured into the world of manual features. As soon as the button was clicked, the video appeared terrible, far from the one in auto mode. I spent hours trying to understand why my image was so blue.

Those early travel films taught me the importance of pacing. They taught me how visuals could evoke a sense of music and how you could build emotion with a well-timed cut or a lingering shot. They also taught me to observe. To really look - not just with my eyes, but through the lens of how something might translate on screen.

I didn't know it at the time, but those were the first seeds of cinematography.

## Building up my cinematography portfolio

After finally figuring out how my camera worked, I could stop wrestling with the beast and start riding it - creatively, shaping the world the way I saw it in my head.

This wasn't about gear - fancy lenses or rigs - it was about the basics, the bones of cinematography: light, movement, composition, story. Tools? Sure, I had a Nikon D3400 and a Zhiyun Crane Weebill gimbal, wobbly at first but does the job.

The difference was that this time, it wasn't just point-and-shoot - it was motivated. That was me, a rookie in India in late 2021, chasing shadows and rickshaw dust, learning to see before I ever touched a London set. I learned by coming up with simple, short film ideas: character, conflict, action to resolve the conflict, and an end. I built on this to figure out my style, learn from the basics, keeping it lean. In this time, I made around 10 short films, out of which 2 were watchable to a third person.

## First Frames: Man in the Mirror

Late 2021, I'm 22, cooped up in my Chandigarh flat, monsoon's over, air sticky, ideas itching. I scribble Man in the Mirror - simple: a guy in his mid-20s stares at his reflection, hates his dead-end life as an engineering student (character); he's trapped in a loop of wanting to break out of his cycle, but his mother forces him to continue down his path as it is traditional (conflict); He realises he's more than that and leaves home (action); ends grinning at dawn (resolution). I hope you're not laughing; this was as simple as it could get, and I had the power to make it visually interesting.

I used so many self-made techniques and rigs for shots I visualised. I storyboarded and shot exactly what I drew. I used a VCR to merge with his dreams; I learnt to play around with shutter speed.

Budget? Zero - me, a cracked bathroom mirror, and my cousin, Aaryaman, playing the distressed engineering student. The Nikon is on a shaky chair supported by a piece of cardboard. Weebill in hand for walkaways. No lights, just a window, and a 60W bulb.

Ten shorts, the rest? Trash - overexposed blurs, static snoozes. But those two? They taught me cinematography's heart: it's not the D3400's sensor or Weebill's motors - it's seeing the light's play, feeling a story's rhythm. Back then, I had no clue about f-stops - guessed, cursed, learned. The Nikon forced focus - kit lens zoomed, I'd stalk the shot. The Weebill demanded patience - hours balancing it, cursing its wobble, till I danced with it. London's MetFilm and The Grandmaster came later - '22, '23 - but India's dust and dusk lit the spark. I shaped what I saw - grief in a crack, grit in a chase - no budget, just vision.

## Actionable Lessons: What My Stumbles Teach You

Note: This is before I relearned the fundamentals I had taught myself; this is my learnings and what helped me before I got the answers from someone else.

Here's my desi playbook from those Nikon days - cinematography's basics, no fancy tools needed:

See Light, Not Gear: Tools don't shoot - your eye does.

This might sound cringey, but honestly, it's true. Currently, in an age with endless camera equipment and endless possibilities, you can literally achieve anything you want to.

But taking from Scorsese, tools help, don't shape.

I came across an interview with Sudeep Chatterjee, the Indian cinematographer behind Bajirao Mastani and Chak De! India. His words hit me: "When you frame a shot, make conscious decisions. Should this be the angle? Why this angle? What does it portray? Why not a different lens?" He said that every answer shapes your style—that's what sets you apart as a DOP. It wasn't about gear; it was about thinking through every choice. That stuck with me and changed how I worked.

Back in India, I was clueless with my Nikon D3400 - shooting rickshaws and street scenes without a plan. Man in the Mirror? I went tight on Aaryaman's eyes because the background looked more blurry on a longer lens - no real reasoning - pure instinct, I would say.

Sudeep's point was clear: instinct's fine, but you've got to question it. Why that frame? What's it doing? I'd been coasting, letting the camera lead. His advice made me rethink everything.

Always know the WHY.

On "The Other Brother," I started applying it. That fight scene - grass flying, fists swinging - I set an Aperture 1200D key light as the backlight because, in every painting I've ever seen of a person in power, specifically in churches, they always had a backlight. This backlight was key in automatically making someone look like a hero.

Add in a low-angle shot at 200 FPS with a subtle eyelight, and you've got yourself a hero shot. I used a 50mm prime to keep it tight on his face, not a 24mm wide that'd scatter the focus. Sudeep's voice was in my head: "Why this? Why not that?" I had answers now - choices, not guesses.

After that interview, I tested it more - shooting a busker in Camden with a borrowed Sony Fx3. The Dutch tilt angle was used because it fit his off-beat vibe, showing a sense of struggle. 35mm lens to catch his face and some background, not an 85mm that'd cut the street out. Sudeep taught me to ask why - what's the shot saying? That's how my style grew- not just shooting, but deciding. It's what makes a DOP, not just a guy with a camera.

In India, I wasn't formally trained in camera and picked it up as a hobby. As soon as I was In Met, I soaked up theoretical knowledge of cinema cameras specifically. I wasn't drawn to AC'ing, so I took the lighting route instead by starting as a spark. You've already read through how I got my first gig as a spark; this chapter covers how I learnt the fundamentals of lighting and camera and applying my learnings.

At MetFilm School, I specialised in Producing and Cinematography. In my cinematography module, I was extremely nervous to meet the tutor. He was a Chinese cinematographer, Zac.

Now I'm unsure if Zac knows this, but he is one of those people in my life that would be a part of my Oscar speech.

He was subtle, to the point, and practical. I took advantage of that. He taught me multiple tips and tricks on how to make the most out of my camera with its settings, lenses, and lighting. We didn't focus on composition and movement.

Sekonic L-858D Speedmaster was my best friend every time I stepped onto the set. It was a superpower I had. Now, Zac was the one who taught me how to use one of these beasts. Here's how Zac broke it down, lesson bylesson, and how it stuck with me.

# Lesson 1: Reading Light - What to Check and Where to Point

Zac's first session with the light meter took place in a MetFilm studio, a bare room with concrete walls, and one Arri 650 tungsten unit blasting a mannequin head. I'd been sparking by then - hauling cables, taping gels - but exposure? Still a hunch game. He hands me the Sekonic L-858D: "This tells you what's real - stop guessing."

He showed me the basics: incident mode, dome out, measuring light falling on the subject, not bouncing off.

"Point it at the source," he said, nodding at the Arri. I hold it under the mannequin's chin, facing the light f/4, 100 ISO, 1/50th pops up. "That's your key light's truth," Zac says. "Now check the fill." I swing it toward a reflector, bouncing soft light with the same settings. Two stops darker - shadows with detail, not a black hole. The next day, I'm on a student short, dusk fading. Zac's there, watching. I point the Sekonic at the HMI key: f/5.6, 400 ISO, 1/50th. Then, the ambient streetlight fills in: f/2.8. "Check the background, too," he adds.

I aim at the wall - f/1.4 - way underexposed. I flag it later, tightening the shot.

Zac's rule stuck: meter every zone - key, fill, background - point at the source, not the subject. It's not about what I see; it's what the light's doing. That Sekonic became my eyes - every set, I'd map it out, no more praying the frame worked.

Now, you must be wondering what I mean by Lighting Ratios:

## Lesson 2: Calculating Lighting Ratios

Zac didn't stop at readings - he drilled ratios into me, how light balances mood. "Ratios are your story's backbone," he said. Back in the studio, he sets up a classic: an Arri 650 key with a reflector fill.

Key reads f/4, fill f/2 - two stops apart.

A 4:1 ratio (each stop doubles or halves lightf/4 to f/2.8 is 2:1, f/2.8 to f/2 is 4:1). "High contrast," he explains. "Dramatic, moody - think noir."

Then he cranks the reflector closer - fill jumps to f/2.8, 2:1 ratio. "Softer, even - good for comedy or romance." I scribble it - 4:1 for grit, 2:1 for calm, 1:1 for flat chat.

On a Camden gig, a talking head, low-budget doc - I test it.

Key from a Skypanel - f/5.6, 200 ISO, 1/50th

fill from a bounce board/2.8.

2:1 ratio, Zac's soft vibe.

The director wants "edgier" - I cut the fill to f/2, 4:1, shadows deepen, and face pops. "Better," she nods. Zac's there later, reviewing: "Know your intent - ratios set the tone." I start metering every setup - key-to-fill, key-to-background - calculating stops on the Sekonic's screen. It's math, sure - f/8 to f/4 is 4:1 - but it's also a feel. That superpower allowed me to dial in drama or ease with no guesswork, just numbers I could trust.

## Lesson 3: Ditch the Monitor - Know Your Camera

Zac hated monitors - well, over-relying on them. "If you know your camera and settings, the meter's enough," he'd say.

We're in a Shoreditch basement - Sony FS7, 50mm prime, me sparking but itching to shoot. He sets an LED key - f/4, 400 ISO, 1/50th - fill at f/2. I peek at the monitor - it looks fine.

"Forget that," Zac snaps. "FS7's got a 14-stop range - trust it. The meter's your map; camera's your muscle."

He's right - I'd been babysitting screens, second-guessing. If I nail exposure - key at f/4, fill two stops under - the FS7's sensor handles it, with no clipping and no mush. Monitors are not always calibrated, and they can tell a different picture than what's actually true. I relied on my light meter, not on monitors.

It's a habit now - meter first, trust the gear, and move on.

## Lesson 4: Lighting a Scene - Start with Blocking

Zac's big one: lighting starts with blocking - where they stand, move, feel.

"Don't touch a light till you see the action," he'd say.

We were shooting a mock scene with two actors arguing. Zac makes us watch: one paces; one leans on a table. "Now light it," he says.

I grab the Sekonic - key from an Arri 1K on the pacer - f/5.6, 200 ISO, 1/50th - angled to catch his stride.

Fill from a reflector on the leaner - f/2.8, 2:1 ratio, tension in the gap.

Background? Window light - f/2 - flagged to f/1.4, darkens the fight's edge. "Why there?" Zac asks. "Pacer's the focus - key follows him," I say. He nods - "Blocking drives it."

Now, this also taught me an important lesson on what I can and can't control and how I need to work around it.

The main element you cannot control on a set is the sun.

So how do you work around this?

You light accordingly. You place your camera where you want it and adjust the aperture based on what the sun is telling you. If it's overexposed, then compensate by lowering the aperture or adding in an ND filter and then blasting up the interior lights to make up for the lost stops.

Start with the sun, then light your way in.

## Key Takeaways: What I Learned from the Grind

Alright, so I've been through the wringer, starting with a Nikon D3400 in India, fumbling my way to MetFilm School, and soaking up gold from my tutor, Zac. The text you gave me? It's a treasure chest of lessons, and I'm breaking it down, desi-style, into what stuck with me. These aren't just notes. They're the stuff that turned me from a clueless kid pointing a camera at ceiling fans to someone who could light a set with confidence. Here's what I'd tell you, fresh and real.

### 1.It Starts with Wanting to See, Not Just Shoot

The big one? My love for cameras kicked off because I couldn't stand forgetting moments, family trips, random street vibes, and the way the light hits a palm leaf. It wasn't about gear or looking cool;

it was about holding onto what I saw. That's the spark: cinematography isn't owning a camera; it's needing to capture life. You don't need a fancy kit to get started; you just need curiosity. I learned that early, before I knew an f-stop from a flop, I was chasing shots because they mattered to me. That's your first step: care enough to look, really look, and the rest follows.

## 2. Gear's Just a Tool Know It Inside Out

The Nikon D3400 wasn't a beast; it was basic, entry-level, and nothing to flex about. But figuring it out auto to manual, why my shots went blue, was like cracking a code. Once I got it, I wasn't fighting the camera; I was using it to shape what I wanted. Lesson here? Master what you've got, cheap or not, before dreaming of upgrades. Know your settings and your limits so you're not guessing when the moment hits. It's not about the price tag; it's about making the tool bend to your will.

## 3. Simple Stories Build Your Eye

Those early shorts, character, conflict, and action end were my playground. Only two out of ten weren't trash, but even the flops taught me pacing, mood, and how a cut can lift a shot. You don't need a big budget or script, just a small idea you can twist visually. Start lean: a guy stuck, a chase, a quiet win. It's less about perfection and more about training your brain to see a story in frames. That's where style creeps; keep it basic; keep it yours.

## 4. Question Every Frame Thanks, Sudeep

Sudeep Chatterjee's interview was a game-changer don't just shoot, think. Why this angle? Why this lens? What's it saying? I used to pick shots because they "felt right," but he made me grill myself. Low angle for power, tight lens for focus, every choice has a reason. That's your style's backbone; it's what makes your work scream "you" instead of "random DOP 5." Next time you frame, ask why five times if you have to until the answers feel solid.

## 5. Light Meters Are Your TruthZac's Gospel

Zac and that Sekonic L-858D? Pure gold. He taught me it's not about what I think I see. It's what the light's actually doing. Point it at the source key, fill the background, and get the numbers: f/5.6, f/2.8, whatever. It's your map, no guesswork. I'd walk onto sets with it like a lifeline, mapping every zone. Do you want control? Meter, know the light's story before you roll. It's not flashy; it's power in your pocket.

## 6. Ratios Set the VibeDial It In

The lighting ratio is 4:1 for drama and 2:1 for chillZac, which drilled that into me. Key at f/4, fill at f/2? That's high contrast and edgy. Bump the fill to f/2.8; it's softer and calmer. It's math; it sure stops doubling or halving, but it's how you tune the mood. Want grit? Cut the fill. Want ease? Balance it. I learned to tweak sets on the fly, and directors loved it. Get a meter and play with ratios; it's your shortcut to nailing tone.

## 7. Trust Your Camera, Skip the Screen

Zac's monitor hate was spot-on: if you know what your camera says, an FS7's 14-stop range, and your settings, you don't need to babysit playback. Meter at f/4, fill two stops under? It'll hold no clipping, no mush. Monitors lie sometimes uncalibrated, tricky but numbers don't. I stopped second-guessing and trusted the gear and my prep. You'll save time and headaches. Set it, check it, roll with it.

## 8. Blocking Your Blueprint Light Later

Zac's rule: watch the action first where; they move, stand, breathe then light it. Pacer gets the key, leaner gets the fill; background's secondary. It's not random blocking that tells you what matters. I'd see directors shift talent, and adjust; key follows the star, while fill keeps it real. Start there; don't touch a light till you know the dance. It's practical, keeps you focused story first, and glow second.

## 9. Sun's BossWork Around It

Biggest Zac takeaway: you can't fight the sun. Overexposed? Drop the aperture, slap an ND filter, and crank interior lights to match. Start with what's outside meter it, and set your base then to build in. It's a hustle, but it's real sun's free light; use it smartly. I'd tweak shots based on daylight, not against it. Learn that early; it's your anchor on any set.

## 10. Stumbles Are Your Guru

Those ten short-sighted duds, two keepers? The trash pile taught me more than the wins. Overexposed skies and shaky pans every flop showed me what not to do. Don't fear screwing up; it's how you grow. Shoot, fail, tweak, rinse and repeat. That's the desi way, jugaad your skills till they stick.

## Why It Matters

These takeaways aren't just tech tricks—they're how I went from a kid with a Nikon in Mumbai to a spark in London who could hold his own. It's not about the gear you buy or the sets you land; it's the why, the how, the grit. Sudeep made me think; Zac made me measure - together, they built my eye.

# How to Enter the Camera Department and Climb to the Top: A Cinematographer's Playbook

So, you want to be a Director of Photography, the best one in the world.

Bold goal. But that's exactly how it should be. In an industry overflowing with DPs, the only thing that separates the greats from the rest is clarity of vision and persistence of action.

When it comes to production roles, it's about hustle, organisation, and being reliable. But the camera department? That's a whole different beast. It's far more creative and because of that, the way in is also more fluid, more chaotic, and honestly, more exciting.

Let's break this down. I'll show you exactly how to get your foot in the door, climb the ladder, build your name, and eventually, if you put in the hours, become one of the best in the game. This is a universal path, but it'll require relentless work, deep observation, and a genuine love for the craft.

## The Entry Point - How to Get Your First Camera Gig

First things first: you don't wait around for someone to give you a chance. You build your chance. Unlike production roles that are slightly more formalised, the camera department is all about reputation, aesthetic, and how you see the world. That starts now.

Before the Roles, Know Yourself.

Before you even think about getting on set or learning what a 2nd AC does, there's something way more important: you need to know who you are and how you see the world. Whether you realise it or not, the way you perceive people, light, texture, colours, chaos, and calm is what shapes the kind of cinematographer you'll become.

During my time in the UK, I've spoken and worked with the world's best DOPs, and this chapter includes what I've learnt from them.

Look, every project has its own visual language. What works for a gritty short film about grief might not work for a fashion ad shot in Morocco.

But underneath it all, you, the DOP, are the ones making choices.

Choices about mood, camera movement, framing, and lensing stem from your perspective. So, before you study techniques, ask yourself: What do I find beautiful? What kind of stories move me? What compositions feel right to me? That's your fingerprint.

You don't need to have it all figured out today. But the earlier you start observing yourself; what you like, what you don't like, what visuals make your heart race, the clearer your vision becomes, and trust me, directors can see when a DOP brings intention to their work. It's not about copying someone else's style. It's about refining your own eye so that when the time comes to serve a story, you're not guessing - you're instinctively translating your worldview through the lens.

So, take time to explore. Shoot for yourself. Reflect. Your identity behind the camera starts with who you are off it. That's the real foundation. One of the most important things to realise early on - your influences don't need to come from other cinematographers. They don't even need to come from film. The stuff that ends up shaping your style can come from literally anywhere: painting, sculpture, street photography, music videos, furniture design, architecture, and lighting in a hotel lobby you once walked through at midnight. It's all fair game.

Take Frank Ockenfels III, the photographer; his work feels cinematic in a way that most moving images don't. What's wild about Ockenfels is that his influences clearly spill out from strange places: abstract painting, mixed-media sketchbooks, weird dreamlike lighting. His portraits aren't just about the subject; they're about the inner world of the subject. You look at one of his photographs, and it feels like a frame from a film that doesn't exist yet, but you want to see it. That's influence. That's voice.

And that's the point. When you're finding your style, don't just binge-watch Roger Deakins's breakdowns and call it research. Go to a gallery. Sit in a brutalist building and feel what the concrete does to your mood. Scroll through old National Geographic covers. Watch how the sun hits a café window. Let that stuff get into your head. That's how your eye develops. You start noticing contrast; differently; you start gravitating toward certain colours, certain kinds of shadows. And slowly, without even trying, you start to build a style that's not borrowed but born.

You want to be the kind of DOP people, remember? Show them something that's uniquely yours. Pull from everywhere. Be unapologetically curious. Because influence isn't just what you watch, it's also what you notice.

Once you've figured out your creative style, start learning the technical.

**Entering the camera department**

The easiest entry-level role is as a Camera Trainee or 2nd AC (Assistant Camera) on short films, commercials, music videos, or student projects. The first few jobs you land won't come from job boards; they'll come from networking, direct messaging people, visiting sets, or simply showing up and offering to help. Even if you're not touching the camera right away, being physically close to it matters. You learn the etiquette, you see how a DP interacts with a gaffer, you learn what not to do, and that's a whole education in itself.

A lot of people confuse a DOP to only be creative handling the visuals but forget that he/she also has a team to manage within a project. He needs to delegate and be aware of how every department bleeds into the visuals. There's a lot of leadership involved.

I got my first real exposure to camera roles just by being present on shoots, helping out where I could, asking questions without being annoying, and staying late. Every DP remembers the person who made their life easier on set.

Get good at being invisible and valuable at the same time. That's your job as a camera trainee. Carry batteries. Log footage. Learn lens sizes like your life depends on them. And always, always keep an eye on the DP's monitor. Ask yourself, "Why that lens? Why that lighting? What mood are they creating?" You're already learning.

Apart from learning the creative side of cinematography, there's another world you must dive into if you want to get consistent work, and that's the technical side.

In fact, I'd go as far as saying that your understanding of camera tech will be the first reason a Director of Photography (DOP) will hire you. Not your vibe. Not your visual references. Not even your taste. Your technical readiness.

Why? Because on set, reliability matters. And someone who knows how to build and maintain a camera from scratch without hesitation is gold.

So, how do you get there? This chapter breaks down exactly how to approach the technical journey, one step at a time, and how it will serve you on real sets with real budgets, where time = money, and mistakes can cost the entire production. The simple things that people normally overlook get you nervous about being on set, but if you know what you're doing, you should be good.

**1. Learn How to Build a Camera from Scratch**

This should be your first and most sacred skill.

Let's say you're hired as a 2nd AC or trainee. The DOP walks in, looks at you, and asks for a handheld setup with wireless video, ND filters, follow focus, and a monitor for the director. You panic. You fumble. You start Googling "How to rig an Arri Alexa with a Hi-5 hand unit." It's over. You've already lost the trust.

Instead, you want to be the person who's so familiar with camera builds that you can see the rig in your head before it's even touched. Arri Alexa Mini LF? Okay, internal NDS, top handle, Teradek for wireless video, Tilta Nucleus for wireless focus, V-Mount battery on the back, EVF extension bracket, matte box... you know it all.

Not just for Arri, but REDs, Sony FX6/FX9, Canon C500, Blackmagic URSA - whatever comes your way.

**How to Learn**: If you haven't gone to film school, start with YouTube: Check out channels like CVP, LensProToGo, or Potato Jet - but go deep into their rig builds behind-the-scenes and camera tests. Another good resource is Arri's free camera menu simulator. You can simply run it on your phone and navigate through the menu as if it were the actual camera.

Assist on indie shoots: Offer to help with student films, passion projects, or low-budget music videos where you can actually touch the camera and get hands-on practice. Build it yourself: If possible, rent a camera and its accessories for a day. Try different configurations: handheld, tripod, gimbal, car rig, etc. Trust me when I say that looking at a tutorial and seeing gear in person is a different game altogether. You need to build a camera physically, tear it down, and know exactly what you did so that if you need to strip down individual components, you know exactly where to start.

Read manuals: No, seriously. Learn to love camera manuals. They're boring, but they'll teach you what even some experienced ACs don't know. Be the geek that people hate to listen to but can't live without when there's a camera error.

## 2. Understand Camera Accessories and Why They Matter

Cameras aren't one-piece tools unless you're shooting with a point-and-shoot with autofocus. They're modular beasts. The difference between a chaotic shoot and a smooth one often comes down to camera build logic.

**Ask yourself:** Are we shooting handheld? Do we need the lightest build? Do we need a wireless video for the director? Should we prioritise battery life or weight?

There have been way too many times that I have built a rig only to realise that it's going to be on a steadicam the whole day and that it doesn't fit. Know the end goal and work backward.

Being able to strip the camera down for a tight gimbal shot and then rebuild it in 10 minutes for a tripod setup with a zoom lens and remote monitor is a skill that makes you invaluable.

**Must-Know Accessories:**

Follow Focus (manual & wireless)
Most commonly used on sets:
Arri Follow Focus FF-5 / FF-4 / FF-1 - Manual
Teradek RT (formerly RTMotion) - Wireless
Preston FIZ (Preston Cinema Systems) - Wireless
Tilta Nucleus-M - Wireless
ARRI Hi-5 - Wireless

Matte Box – Holds filters and blocks light leaks.

ND Filters – Helps control exposure without compromising f-stop.

Wireless Transmitters (Teradek, Hollyland) – Sends live image feed to director/clients.

External Monitors – For 1st AC, Director, or DOP.
Most commonly used on sets:
SmallHD Cine 7 | SmallHD 1303 HDR / Cine 13
Atomos Shogun CONNECT / Ninja Ultra
TVLogic F-7H MK2

Power Systems (V-Mount, Gold Mount, D-Tap Splitters) – Knowing power flow is vital for avoiding shutdowns mid-shot.

Pro Tip: Learn what breaks first. Loose BNC cables, overheating SSDs, and HDMI handshake issues - when these things happen on set, being the one who calmly solves them = a big win.

## 3. Know How to Prep Like a Pro

Camera prep is an art form. It's what separates amateur chaos from professional calm. When you go into a rental house or prep day, your job is to double, triple check everything. You're lucky if you do get a prep day on a job, so it's wise to learn this before you get booked for a project.

**Here's a proper camera prep checklist:**

All accessories tested and working.
All cables labelled and correctly routed.
Lens mounts are tightened and clean.
Wireless systems paired and calibrated.
Media formatted and properly labelled.
Batteries charged and chargers packed.
Camera timecode synced if there are multiple units.

Ensure you can quickly change a lens, especially if your rig is designed in a way that restricts access to the lens. You should know how long each task takes and what tools you'll need on your belt to do them fast.

**Pro tip:** If you want to go pro, buy yourself a solid tool belt. Fill it with lens cleaners, a multi-tool, sharpies, Allen keys, lens cloths, zip ties, and some gaffer tape. These small tools make you feel like Batman on set.

### 4. Learn Exposure and Monitoring Tools

Knowing how to judge exposure isn't just an "eye" thing. It's technical, too. On high-end sets, you'll need to understand waveforms, false colours, zebras, and histograms. DOPs and gaffers trust their monitors, scopes, and meters, and so should you.

**Key tools:**

False Colour: Learn what 18% grey looks like. Memorise skin tone zones.

Waveform: Tells you if your shot is over- or underexposed across the frame.

Zebra Stripes: Great for quick exposure alerts - often used on Sony systems.

Light Meter: Not essential for every shoot, but using one can help you really understand ratios between key, fill, and background.

This level of precision is what makes you go from "I like this" to "I know this works."

## 5. Match Your Technical Skills to the Story

This is more for a DOP to decide and then communicate to you accordingly.

All the gear and tech knowledge in the world means nothing if you don't know when and why to use it. That's what separates a gearhead from a real cinematographer.

Let's say the story is about a lonely man in a city. You wouldn't shoot it on a gimbal with wide lenses at golden hour. Maybe it's handheld. Maybe it's longer lenses with shallow depth to isolate the character. You build the rig accordingly, small, light, and stripped down. Or a big-budget action film? You might have three rigs prepped: one for high-speed car chases, one for interiors, and one for stunt rigs. All are built to precision, with fast hot-swapping in mind.

The point is: Your tech knowledge should serve the story. You're not flexing with a Steadicam just to look cool. You're using what works because you've done the work to understand it.

## Start Shooting - The Only Way to Get Noticed

The fastest, realistic way to break into cinematography is simple: just shoot.

Shoot, like your life depends on it. Shoot, like the only thing standing between you and your dream is another frame, another setup because it is. The more you shoot, the more you learn. But more importantly, the more you shoot and share, the more people get to know your style. That's how you get noticed.

This is where music videos come in. I cannot stress this enough: music videos are the playground of every young cinematographer.

They're short and expressive, and often, you can work with musicians who are just as hungry as you. DM singers on Instagram and reach out to artists looking to promote a single. You don't need a budget, just an idea, a vibe, and a team that wants to make something cool.

Shoot five music videos. One per week if you can. By the fifth, you'll have started to find your style. You'll know what you like - soft light, harsh contrast, handheld, slick dolly shots, shallow depth, or deep focus. These early videos are less about perfection and more about taste. The more you do, the faster you'll realise where your eye naturally goes. Give the footage to your mate to edit. Collaborate. Experiment. But always shoot with intention. Shoot as if a future director is watching and thinking, "Yeah… I want that look."

## Getting Seen: How to Show Your Work and Get Booked

So you've started finding your eye, you're shooting regularly, your visuals are getting sharper, and now comes the hard part: getting people to notice. Because in this game, it's not just about how good you are. It's about how easy it is for people to remember you when they need someone to shoot their next thing.

Let's break it down.

**Shoot. Share. Repeat.**

This sounds basic, but I mean it: you need to keep shooting and keep sharing. Don't just wait for the perfect project - go out and create work that speaks to your style. Music videos, spec ads, mood reels, whatever. Do it scrappy if you have to, but just get it done. Every time you finish a piece, put it out there. Not with a "look at me" vibe, but with a clear sense of: this is what I see, and this is what I bring to the table.

Post to Instagram, TikTok, and LinkedIn - but tailor each one. Instagram is your gallery. Treat it like a mood board of your aesthetic. Clean grid, high-quality stills, color consistency. Use Reels to break down your process (bts + final).

- TikTok is where you can show your personality. Tell stories behind the shoots, show lighting setups, camera tests, and what inspired you.

- LinkedIn is where producers, coordinators, and directors are watching. Post about the job after it's done; talk about what you learned on set, how you problem-solved, how your visual style evolved.

## The key: Consistency over virality. Keep showing up.

Gawx is a standout example of a creative who seamlessly blends visual artistry with cinematic storytelling. Known for his distinctive style, he brings a painter's eye to the world of cinematography, crafting visuals that are both striking and emotionally resonant. His work is characterised by meticulous attention to colour, composition, and lighting, resulting in imagery that feels both intentional and evocative.

On Instagram, Gawx shares not just his finished projects but also behind-the-scenes insights, offering a glimpse into his creative process. This transparency not only showcases his technical skills but also his commitment to storytelling and visual innovation. His ability to transform everyday scenes into cinematic moments has garnered a substantial following, reflecting the impact of his unique approach to filmmaking.

### 2. Make a Showreel That Actually Hits

Your showreel isn't a montage; it's a statement.

- Keep it under 90 seconds.
- Don't just throw clips together and edit to a rhythm; show range within your style.

- Group work by tone (moody, natural, commercial, etc.) and start strong. You want people to feel something in the first 10 seconds, or they're clicking out.
- If your reel is mid? Cool. Keep shooting and update it every 3 months.

Then, link it everywhere. Your email signature, your Instagram bio, your WhatsApp status. Dead serious. Make it stupidly easy for someone to find your work.

**3. Your Network Is Your Net Worth**

This is where most people drop the ball. Your next job is probably coming from someone you already know or someone they know. So, build real relationships. Here's how:

- Go to film festivals, Q&As, and gear expos. Not to network in a fake way but to talk to people about things you both love. If someone made a short you liked, go up and say it. If a Dop lights something in a cool way, ask them how they did it. Be human. People remember that.

- DM other camera people, ACs, and producers on Instagram or LinkedIn. Don't beg for a job; just say you like their work and ask if they're open to grabbing a coffee sometime.

- Stay in touch without being annoying. If you shoot something new, send it to them with a one-liner: "Hey! Just wrapped this one - thought you might like the look."

And here's a big one, Don't wait for permission.

If you see someone you want to work with - a director, a small brand, a musician - pitch them directly. Send them a message like:

> *"Hey, I'm a cinematographer, and I love the tone of your last project. If you're working on anything new, I'd love to collaborate; I'm building out my reel and happy to work around your budget."*

That one message? It can lead to five jobs. That's how I started.

### 4. Get Credited Everywhere

You shot something? Make sure you're tagged, credited, and findable. When people repost the video, ask them to tag you. If they forget, remind them. Not in an egoistic way - just say, "It really helps with my visibility." Most people will do it. It takes two seconds.

Upload your work to Vimeo. Credit the crew in your captions. Create a Notion or Google Doc with all your credits. Start thinking like a professional early. Makes a big difference when people start asking for your CV.

## 5. Use Downtime Strategically

When you're not shooting, you're not "free" - you're in R&D mode. Watch films with the sound off. Break down lighting setups. DM the other camera crew and ask if you can shadow them on set. Offer to be a 2nd AC or even a runner on camera-heavy shoots. It's all an experience. And every set you step onto is a door to the next one.

> TL;DR - Want More Camera Gigs?
> - Keep shooting, keep sharing
> - Make a reel that hits emotionally
> - Build genuine relationships, not contacts
> - Stay visible, stay humble, stay hungry
> - Turn every job into five new ones

This is how you turn your camera work into a career. If you do this for six months with intention, you will get noticed. Keep doing it for five years? You're dangerous. Ten years? You're a name people say in rooms you're not even in. You don't always have to climb the ladder from 1st AC to DP; you can start shooting directly; there is no one way. But if you do want to learn the department inside out, here is how you climb the ladder.

## Climbing the Ladder – 1st AC to DP

Now, if you want to learn the craft from the inside out, another path (alongside shooting your own projects) is climbing the traditional ladder:

Camera Trainee

2nd AC (Clapper Loader)

1st AC (Focus Puller)

Camera Operator

Director of Photography

Working through these roles on larger sets teaches you discipline, workflow, and crew coordination. You learn about gear, lenses, onset hierarchy, and how to lead a camera team. It also gets you on bigger shoots - TV, commercials, features - which exposes you to how top-tier DPs operate. Even when you're pulling focus, you're learning. You're watching how the DP lights a room, how they speak to the gaffer, how they translate the director's vision.

Some DPs skip this ladder and go straight from indie shorts to DP. Others climb every rung. Both paths are valid. But you have to be consistent. Build your network. Keep your name in people's minds. Get known for your reliability as much as your creativity.

## Timeline to Becoming a Top-Tier DP (And Staying There)

Here's a rough timeline for becoming a world-class cinematographer. Yours may move faster or slower, but this gives you something to aim for:

Year 1 - 2

Shoot everything you can: shorts, passion projects, no-budget music videos
- Work as a trainee or 2nd AC on larger sets
- Build your reel
- Find 2–3 directors you vibe with - grow with them

Year 3 - 4
- Shoot bigger music videos and indie commercials
- Become a go-to DP in your circle
- Start getting agency work or brand content gigs
- Build relationships with production companies
- Experiment with different styles - stretch your limits

Year 5 - 6
- Shoot your first feature or long-form series
- Get signed to a production company or agent

Refine your brand and aesthetic

Speak at workshops or festivals - become a thought leader

Year 7+

Shoot national commercials, international features

Win awards, get festival buzz

Get represented by a major cinematography agency

Inspire the next generation

And throughout this entire journey? Keep shooting. Keep learning. Stay obsessed. Cinematography is the art of storytelling through light, and the best DPs in the world never stop chasing light.

## Influences:
### 1. The Fall (2006) – DOP: Colin Watkinson

"The Fall" is one of those films that feels more like a dream than anything resembling traditional storytelling. Directed by Tarsem Singh, this visually stunning fantasy tells the story of a young girl and a bedridden stuntman who weaves an epic tale. What's remarkable about "The Fall" is how it plays with both visual storytelling and the idea of cinema as a spectacle. It's a film that requires you to pay attention not just to the plot but to the carefully constructed world in which it's set.

## Composition & Camera Movement

The use of color is almost overwhelming, but in the best way possible. Each frame seems to be an isolated artwork, from the vibrant reds of the desert to the lush green of the jungle. The camera is always in motion, whether it's sweeping across sprawling landscapes or lingering over delicate details like the subtle glint of light in an eye. What I find truly fascinating is the use of wide-angle lenses to exaggerate space, which creates a heightened sense of drama and fantasy.

For those looking to explore unique compositions, this film is a goldmine. Every shot is meticulously framed, and each foreground element is exaggerated to create a surreal feeling. It's like entering a world where reality is not governed by conventional rules, something I'd love to experiment with more in my own work

## Colour & Texture

One of the things that stays with you after watching "The Fall" is the masterful use of colour. Every single scene feels like an oil painting, bold and emotionally evocative. Tarsem Singh uses saturated hues to highlight emotions, but he never overdoes it. It's never gaudy or artificial, just rich, expressive, and tangible.

This is a fantastic lesson in creating a sense of place without being obvious or relying solely on CGI. I want to take this approach into my own work - how can I make a simple setting feel larger than life through the lens and lighting alone?

## 2. Enter the Void (2009) – DOP: Benoît Debie

"Enter the Void" is a wildly experimental film by Gaspar Noé, shot by the talented Benoît Debie, and it is not for everyone. But if you're a cinematographer or visual artist looking to push boundaries, it's a must-see. The film's structure and visuals are dreamlike and often jarring, in-your-face. It's about a drug dealer's experiences in the afterlife, exploring themes of consciousness, life, and death. But beyond the story, the film's visuals are mind-bending in their use of light, perspective, and fluidity.

**Camera Movement & Unusual Shots**

What I love about "Enter the Void" is how the camera almost never stays still. There's a constant flow, much like the protagonist's journey through different states of being. The film's POV shots are disorienting, especially when the camera floats, simulating a disembodied soul traveling through space. One of the most iconic shots is when the camera travels through a neon-lit city, mimicking the sensation of being "high" or "tripping." The camera movements are an extension of the protagonist's unstable, surreal experiences. It's not just a gimmick; everything about the camera movement immerses you deeper into the experience.

This is something I would love to experiment with, how the camera can be more than a passive observer but an active participant in the emotional experience. Moving the camera in a way that directly reflects the mind of the character is a lesson that I plan on incorporating in future projects.

**Lighting & Color**

The colour palette in "Enter the Void" is bold and psychedelic, often flickering with neon pinks, blues, and yellows, which can be overwhelming at times. The lighting is often surreal and ethereal, casting glows or playing with shadow in ways that heighten the sense of disorientation and altered perception. I've been fascinated by how lighting can transform a simple scene into one that is infused with emotional and psychological depth. "Enter the Void" is a film where the lighting and color are not just stylistic choices but integral to the story itself.

## 3. The Duke of Burgundy (2014) – DOP: Nikos Aliagas

This film, directed by Peter Strickland, is an unusual mix of eroticism, psychological drama, and surrealism. Set in a world that feels almost timeless, the story revolves around the complex and intense relationship between two women, but it's the film's visuals that stand out as an unconventional and unique way to tell this story.

## Composition & Framing

The framing of shots in "The Duke of Burgundy" feels highly intentional, with elements often off-center, sometimes too tight or too far away, creating a sense of unease or intimacy, depending on the moment. The camera lingers almost uncomfortably on the characters as if asking you to read between the lines of their interactions. The compositions often employ symmetrical framing, which gives each scene a highly stylized feel, almost as if each one is a painting in itself. This is definitely something I could adopt in my own work, experimenting with balance and tension in the composition.

## Lighting & Atmosphere

What truly elevates "The Duke of Burgundy" is the atmospheric lighting. Instead of relying on bright, natural daylight, Nikos Aliagas creates soft, muted lighting that gives everything a vintage, almost nostalgic feel. The lighting is so specific and integral to the mood of the film that it's easy to imagine the characters' emotions without them needing to say much at all. The colour choices (rich reds, deep purples, warm browns) all contribute to an underlying tension that builds and builds. The whole film feels like a slowly boiling pot, and the lighting brings that feeling to life.

# 4. The Holy Mountain (1973) – DOP: Alejandro Jodorowsky

"The Holy Mountain," directed by the ever-provocative Alejandro Jodorowsky, is a surrealist film known for its shocking and controversial imagery. It's not the kind of movie you watch casually; it's more like an experience, one that pushes the boundaries of what cinema can do. While the film itself can be difficult to sit through for many, it remains a fascinating exploration of symbolism, color, and form.

**Composition & Symbolism**

The compositions in "The Holy Mountain" are a mixture of chaotic and calculated. Every frame is filled with surreal, often religious, symbolism. Jodorowsky uses wide shots to show vastness and isolation, while tight shots evoke a sense of suffocation and confinement. The film is full of disorienting transitions between the bizarre and the mundane. There's a sense that the world of the film is in constant flux, and the way the camera moves and shifts feels almost like it's trying to keep up with the insanity.

**Color & Lighting**

Like "Enter the Void," the use of colour in "The Holy Mountain" is meant to be jarring. Bright, garish colours flood the screen, creating an uncomfortable visual experience. The lighting is stark, sometimes high-contrast, with deep shadows and intensely lit faces that create a sense of otherworldliness. It's almost as though Jodorowsky was determined to make you feel the strangeness of the film visually, not just through the narrative. For me, this is a perfect reminder of how colour and light can not only evoke emotion but shape the viewer's understanding of the narrative itself.

## 5. A Ghost Story (2017) – DOP: Andrew Droz Palermo

"A Ghost Story" might not seem like an unconventional pick at first glance. The film, directed by David Lowery, is a slow-burn, meditative piece about love, loss, and the passage of time. However, the way the cinematography enhances the film's themes is truly unique. It's a perfect example of how a minimalist, deliberate visual style can elevate a narrative that's both simple and profound.

**Composition & Camera Movement**

The most striking feature of "A Ghost Story" is its use of stillness and time. There are extended shots where nothing moves, and no one speaks. The camera is static, observing the world, letting time pass. It's a brilliant use of the slow-paced, almost lethargic pace of life. By holding long, unbroken shots, the cinematography allows the audience to process the weight of the moment and feel the passage of time in a very real, physical way. I'm always fascinated by the power of holding a shot, and this film taught me how much can be said with just a look.

**Lighting & Atmosphere**

The lighting in "A Ghost Story" is soft, natural, and often dim. The haunting, ethereal quality of the lighting matches the film's themes of ghosts and memories. It's a reminder that sometimes less is more. You don't need bright lights to make a scene feel emotionally resonant. It's a lesson I always return to in my own work: how can I tell a story with shadows, with the absence of light, instead of flooding the frame with excessive exposure?

## Final Thoughts

These films all taught me something different, from understanding the importance of movement and composition to realizing how crucial color, lighting, and texture can be in crafting the emotional undertones of a scene. As a cinematographer, I plan to continue pulling from all these influences. But more than anything, I've learned that there's no one way to shoot something the beauty is in discovering what works best for the story you're telling.

Each frame, each decision, is part of a larger picture that builds not just the visual language of the film but the emotional journey of the audience. That's what I aim to capture with my own lens, and it's this constant study of visual storytelling that pushes me forward in my journey as a DOP.

The unusual advice I've picked on along the way

1. **Have your own kit of unique camera toys.**

   You have your own style; you need to have your own little bag of tricks that get you your style. I learned from one of my favorite cinematographers, Mark Barrs, who shared that he had his own little camera kit filled with weird stuff that no one but him and his team could comprehend. This bag was filled with nail polish, women's tights, a dangling string of broken mirrors, and Vaseline. Yes, I know I owe you an explanation - the nail polish and women's tights. That's clear nail polish used to stick a single or sometimes double layer of a milky black pro mist filter at the back of your lens without darkening your image. The dangling mirrors and Vaseline are for when you just need a messy frame. You always need something in the foreground, and you may not always have something within the set to achieve the effect you want - of course, only if it's creatively driven, powering the story.

2. **You remember the grad film I shot, "The Other Brother."**

   So, in that film, we had an issue where we couldn't use the haze machine due to the location we were shooting in, and because of that, I couldn't get the look that I wanted for my epic fight scene that had smoke flying around the hero's punches. I was let down by production, but I was persistent in getting my signature look for the scene. My fix? It was a stupid one, but honestly, looking back, it worked. Instead of using a full-blown haze machine that would affect our shooting restriction list, I told one of our crew members who loved vaping to jump in and fill in for our lost machine. Unusual but effective.

The lesson in this one is that your plan will not always go the way you want it to, but don't forget that what matters is the final output. Your goal is to focus on that, not get married to the way you go about achieving it. The first solution is not always the only solution. This can also be applied to many other shoots that I have done, which required quick fixes, such as using car headlights as backlights, a leaf blower for imitating wind, and a clothing line for an aerial dolly, among many more. Fixing a problem has one way you thought of and then a million other ways you could also do it.

### 3. Remember that every frame counts

An extremely important point that many people overlook is that the shots need to be cut together, and if one shot is off, the sequence feels off. Ensure you're consistent throughout.

## The Future of Cinematography

There was a time when the essence of cinematography was firmly rooted in the real world - lights, lenses, locations, and weather. It was about how you captured what was in front of the camera. But that era, while still vital, is no longer the sole playing field. As we move into the future, cinematography is no longer confined to what exists in front of a lens - it's about what can exist, even if it's born inside a machine.

This struck me while I was researching the movie "Dune," shot by cinematographer Greig Fraser. I'm sure you know about how beautiful "Dune" looks, but you might be unaware of what went on behind the scenes.

This was an unusual set for the camera department because they had to work extremely closely with the post-production team.

The green light for anything visual was now up to two people - Greig Fraser and his VFX supervisor, Paul Lambert. If either had an issue, it wasn't possible.

After listening to "Team Deakin's" podcast, I noted that Fraser has said the role of a cinematographer now stretches beyond traditional limits. It's no longer just about showing up on set with a camera and figuring out the lighting. It's about working with digital spaces, game engines, and real-time render tools. It's about lighting virtual environments with the same intentionality you would a physical one.

This completely changes the entire craft of cinematography because it affects everything you need to know about what affects your image in post-production.

## Understanding the New Tools

At the heart of this evolution is software like Unreal Engine, a real-time 3D creation tool developed by Epic Games. Originally built for gaming, it's now at the centre of a revolution in film production, offering filmmakers the power to build and interact with complex worlds before a single frame is shot.

With virtual production, cinematographers can now explore camera angles, pre-light scenes, and even block actors in a digital environment that mimics the physical world. In Fraser's words, "We're not replacing reality; we're enhancing our ability to control it."

This is not just previs; this is cinematography in real-time. In the making of The Mandalorian, Fraser worked with The Volume, a circular array of LED screens powered by Unreal Engine. The innovation allowed the team to create photorealistic backdrops that respond dynamically to camera movement and lens changes.

The result? In-camera VFX that blurs the line between the physical and the digital.

# From Set to Simulation

Traditionally, a cinematographer might scout a desert, wait for a magic hour, and frame a shot. Today, Fraser can walk onto a soundstage in Los Angeles and light a virtual desert in real-time, complete with reactive sunlight, atmospheric haze, and dynamic terrain, all built with Unreal Engine.

Paul Lambert, meanwhile, brings these worlds to life with an eye for realism. His role is no longer just post-production cleanup; it's co-authoring the visual language with the DP from the earliest stages.

"The VFX is no longer an add-on," Lambert has said. "It's part of the narrative, part of the lighting, part of the emotional arc." That collaboration changes everything.

It's not just about pixels; it's about storytelling through digital cinematography.

The symbiosis between Fraser and Lambert embodies what Bordwell and Thompson (2013) describe as the "creative fusion" of cinematography and digital artistry, blurring boundaries between traditionally siloed roles. This co-authorship impacts how narrative meaning is constructed visually, as lighting design and digital effects become inseparable in crafting mood, tone, and emotional resonance (Bazin, 2005). It also aligns with contemporary media theorists' understanding of cinema as an "expanded audiovisual space" where virtual and physical realities coalesce (Manovich, 2001).

The interplay between real-time virtual environments and traditional cinematic principles facilitates new expressive possibilities, enabling filmmakers to tell stories that were previously impossible or prohibitively expensive to realize (Elsaesser, 2019).

In this sense, the future of cinematography is not just about capturing images; it's about shaping immersive worlds and emotional experiences through a digitally augmented creative process, where the visual effects artist and the cinematographer together become authors of the film's visual soul.

## The Rise of the Hybrid Cinematographer

What emerges from this is a new breed of cinematographer: the hybrid artist. They still understand exposure, lenses, grip gear, and natural light, but they're also learning node-based lighting systems, 3D scene assembly, and digital camera emulation.

The camera isn't always physical. Sometimes, it's virtual. But the eye behind it? That still has to be human.

"This might be a bit confusing, but if I asked you whether an animator on a Pixar movie should be called a 'cinematographer,' what would you say?"

Fraser doesn't see the new tools as a threat. "It's not about replacing the cinematographer," he said in an interview. "It's about empowering us to do more to paint with new brushes. "Learning Unreal Engine, or Blender, or working with VAD (Virtual Art Department) is fast becoming as essential as learning how to use a light meter. For the next generation of DPs, these tools aren't optional extras; they're part of the foundation.

## Lighting the Unreal

One of the key shifts is the way we think about lighting. In the physical world, light bounces in predictable ways. It's governed by physics.

But in Unreal Engine, you get both physics and freedom. You can bend the rules. Want a backlight that doesn't affect the background? Easy. Need a fill light that adjusts to a character's movement? Done.

But here's the catch: just because you can do something doesn't mean you should. That's where the DP's taste and restraint come in. Fraser's work proves that the most successful use of virtual cinematography isn't when it shouts; it's when it whispers so convincingly you forget it was ever digital.

It's about maintaining photographic integrity, even when the environment is entirely synthetic.

## Case Study — Dune

In Dune, Fraser and Lambert created some of the most memorable cinematic images of the last decade. The massive sandworms, the brutalist architecture, the infinite deserts, much of it was either enhanced or fully rendered digitally.

But it never felt digital.

The trick, according to Fraser, was integrating VFX into the cinematographic process from day one. He worked closely with Lambert to build previs scenes inside Unreal, test camera moves, and even simulate weather conditions like dust storms and eclipse lighting.

The lighting setups weren't just technical; they were emotional.

The softness of the light on Arrakis told us about the harsh beauty of the desert. The darkness inside the Sardaukar ships hinted at the brutality of war. And every frame felt intentional because the visual effects weren't added later; they were woven into the cinematographic fabric.

## When the LED Wall Becomes a Location

Virtual production allows us to shoot in "locations" that don't exist.

But that doesn't mean the craft is gone. In fact, it might demand more discipline.

With The Volume, you still need to choose lenses. You still need to block actors. You still need to make decisions about color temperature and key-to-fill ratios. You make those choices in an environment that can respond to you in real-time.

This is why Fraser insists that understanding these tools doesn't make you less of a cinematographer; it makes you more capable. Because the final image still comes down to your intuition and your understanding of light and story.

## The New Language of Previz

In traditional production, previsualization (previz) was often used to rough out sequences, especially for action or VFX-heavy scenes.

But now, previz is pre-cinematography.

Fraser uses it to test how lenses will behave in virtual environments, how shadows will fall across digital terrain, and how lighting changes affect mood before stepping on set.

And because it's all happening in a shared space (Unreal Engine) the cinematographer, director, production designer, and VFX team can all work collaboratively in real-time.

This is what Paul Lambert calls "democratising the frame." Everyone can see it. Everyone can contribute. But the DP still leads the visual language.

## What This Means for You

If you're an aspiring cinematographer today, you need to embrace this shift.

That doesn't mean abandoning your knowledge of lenses and lighting. It means expanding your skillset to include tools like Unreal, TouchDesigner, and Nuke.

Learn how virtual cameras behave.
Understand how light works in a 3D space.
Play with simulations. Break the rules. And learn how to bring emotion to digital scenes.

It's no longer just about what camera you own; it's about how you craft a world, even if that world only exists in pixels.

The future belongs to those who can merge art with technology, who can wield virtual light with the same finesse as a 1K Fresnel, and who can compose a shot inside a digital jungle as beautifully as one in a real rainforest.

Greig Fraser and Paul Lambert aren't just working with what's real. They're working with what's possible.

As we step into this new era, the question isn't whether cinematography will survive; it's whether it will thrive. It's whether we're willing to evolve with it. And if you're reading this, chances are, you are.

# Chapter 5 - The Future of Film and where It's heading

Why film is not the same as it was 100 years ago?

Film is still a baby. If you compare it to other art forms - painting, music, theatre, even photography - it's barely crawling. It's just over 100 years old, and yet, somehow, in this tiny window of time, it's become one of the most powerful forms of storytelling humanity has ever known.

This section isn't just about walking you through the history of cinema like a museum tour. You can Google timelines for that. What we're doing here is digging deeper into the why.

Why did filmmakers start cutting between shots? Why did audiences crave sound? What made some directors pick up cameras and shoot in the streets while others leaned into VFX and fantasy? What kinds of problems were people trying to solve, and what did that do to the art form?

Every evolution in film wasn't just about better gear or slicker visuals. It was about a shift in thinking. A rebellion against limitations. A hunger to say something different or to say it in a way no one had before.

That's what this chapter is about: the revolutions of cinema. The moments when someone, somewhere, decided, "Let's do this differently."

Because as a filmmaker, especially today, you're not just inheriting this art form; you're being invited to disrupt it, too.

So, how did it get here? How did we go from grainy black-and-white clips of factory workers walking out of a building to multi-million dollar epics shot across continents and streamed on devices that fit in your pocket?

It all started simple. The first films were short, silent, and barely a few minutes long. No real plot - just moving images: a train pulling into a station (L'Arrivée d'un train en gare de La Ciota), a man sneezing, and a kiss.

This wasn't storytelling yet; it was an exploration of a new scientific discovery. A new way to capture reality. A camera was set up, people walked in and out of frame, and that was it. The Lumière Brothers weren't trying to make a movie; they were showing a marvel.

People gathered just to marvel at the tech: "Whoa! That looks real!" No one had seen motion captured this way before. There was no editing, no narrative. Just observation.

But very quickly, filmmakers realised they could play with time. Cut from one shot to another. Show cause and effect. Tell a story. The thought was: what if we could show something impossible? That was Georges Méliès. A magician-turned-filmmaker who used early editing and in-camera effects to make the moon come alive. He was the first to ask, "What if film isn't just a window to the world but a tool to reshape it?"

That single shift from observation to imagination sparked the creative potential of cinema.

And just like that, the film became art.

## Silent Film & the Invention of Visual Language (1910s–1920s)

As more people gained access to film cameras, something strange began to happen: people started telling stories. Remember, back then, sound wasn't introduced, and without sound, they had to rely on pure visuals. That's where the grammar of film was born. Cross-cutting to show two places at once. Close-ups to show emotion. Wide shots to establish geography. Filmmakers like D.W. Griffith codified these techniques, but others, especially in Germany and the Soviet Union, were pushing visual storytelling to emotional extremes.

German Expressionism distorted reality through its sets and lighting, while Soviet montage theory utilized editing as a powerful emotional tool. These weren't just style choices. They were reactions to war, trauma, and political upheaval. Film was beginning to feel. And with that came power.

This is where the language of the film really took shape. Directors like D.W. Griffith (problematic, yes, but influential) developed editing techniques that allowed audiences to experience emotions such as suspense, longing, and fear. Without sound, every emotion had to come through visuals - lighting, framing, movement. Cinematographers became painters with motion. Actors had to exaggerate everything, and the music (often played live in the theatre) was what tied it all together.

German Expressionism - films like The Cabinet of Dr. Caligari (1920) pushed visual style to the extreme. Angled sets, heavy shadows, surreal worlds. This was the birth of mood in cinema.

## The Sound Revolution (1930s–1950s)

In 1927, everything changed with The Jazz Singer. Suddenly, characters could speak. Sound opened up a whole new layer of storytelling dialogue, score, and ambient sound. But it also meant filmmakers had to rethink everything. Cameras had to be encased to prevent mic interference. The sets had to be quiet. Actors had to adjust their performances. For a while, the visuals actually became less interesting because sound was the shiny new toy.

This period was manic; people were confused, and actors struggled to adapt to the introduction of sound, as a new wave of technology was also being introduced. Still, this period gave us absolute classics. Hollywood's Golden Age was in full swing. Studios like MGM and Warner Bros. were cranking out musicals, noirs, westerns, and comedies like Clockwork. The "studio system" era had begun.

Meanwhile, other countries were experimenting. Italian Neorealism (Bicycle Thieves, 1948) stripped film down to its rawest truth. Real people, real streets, real stories.

## Colour, Scope, and the Spectacle (1950s–1960s)

Television had arrived, and studios were in panic mode. So they fought back with size: widescreen formats, dazzling Technicolour, massive sets. Films like Ben-Hur, The Ten Commandments, and Lawrence of Arabia were renowned for their epic scale and immersive storytelling. It was a way to get people back into cinemas and give them what TV couldn't.

But elsewhere, artists were reacting against this too-polished system. In France, the New Wave was exploding: handheld cameras, jump cuts, improvised performances. Truffaut, Godard, Varda, these weren't just films; they were manifestos.

Each movement in the film was becoming a response, sometimes to culture, sometimes to technology, but always to the status quo. This was cinema's rebellious teenage phase. This was the first time that cinema distribution was questioned, the foundation of online distribution.

## The Auteur Era (1970s–1980s)

In the '70s, something magical happened. The studios started trusting weird young filmmakers. Coppola, Scorsese, Spielberg, Kubrick, Lucas. These were auteurs-directors with a signature style and a strong point of view.

The stories got darker. More personal. Grittier. Films like Taxi Driver, The Godfather, and Apocalypse Now weren't made to make money (though they often did). They were made to say something. Cinematography matured, too. DOPs like Gordon Willis and Vilmos Zsigmond were known for their use of shadows and natural light. You started seeing more handheld work, long takes, and poetic camera moves.

Then came Star Wars and Jaws, and everything changed again. The blockbuster was born.

This era could be known as the one that shaped the fundamentals of storytelling.

## Digital, Indie, and DIY (1990s–2000s)

The 90s were a wild mix. You had slick studio stuff (The Matrix, Titanic), but you also had the rise of indie film. Tarantino, Linklater, PTA. Suddenly, if you had a weird script and a few thousand bucks, you could get into Sundance and maybe even win an Oscar.

Digital cameras started creeping in. At first, people hated the look. But it made filmmaking cheaper, faster, and more democratic. Anyone could shoot something. The gear was evolving rapidly. DV cams. MiniDV. HD. And in the 2000s, RED and ARRI's digital systems would shift the entire industry.

At the same time, visual effects exploded. Films like The Lord of the Rings and Avatar set a new bar for what was possible. Cinema was now blending reality and fantasy seamlessly. This was a revolution of access. A breakdown of hierarchy. Suddenly, the tools of the trade were in everyone's hands.

# Streaming, Social Media & the Fragmentation of Cinema (2010s–Now)

Then came Netflix. And YouTube. And TikTok. And iPhones with cinematic mode.

Now, anyone can shoot a film on their phone, edit it on their laptop, and upload it to the world. The gatekeepers are dissolving. The biggest shift was in the way that we consumed cinema.

In earlier days, film was regarded as a social space where a community could come together and be entertained. The way people watched a film was also affected by the community. Nowadays, watching a film is no longer a social event; it's a solitary one.

The access to watching films flew wide open - there was too much choice. Film has now become a matter of self-regulation. We're also watching films differently, not just in theatres but on laptops, tablets, and even Instagram feeds. This changes the type of stories we tell. Intimate, fast-paced, scroll-stopping.

I was on the Tube the other day when I spotted someone watching Chris Nolan's Interstellar on a 5-inch iPhone screen with no headphones, just subtitles. Let that sink in. A film our dear friend Hoyte van Hoytema shot on 70mm IMAX, meticulously framed to stretch across an eight-storey theatre screen, was now scrunched into a display smaller than a postcard... with the Jubilee Line's finest sound design providing the background score. I nearly dropped my own phone out of second-hand shame.

If Hoytema saw this, I'm pretty sure he'd drop his Leica and just walk into the sea. Imagine spending months crafting celestial visuals with a resolution so crisp it could humble God - only for some guy named Finance Craig to watch it in portrait mode while balancing a Pret sandwich on his knee. This is what I mean when I say the way we "consume" film has changed just as much as the way we make it. A century ago, film was a communal event—a night out with an orchestra playing live under the screen. Now, it's a solitary activity squeezed in between TikTok doomscrolls and missed notifications. And don't get me wrong, I'm not a snob- okay, maybe a little, but there's a difference between evolution and sacrilege.

The point of this chapter isn't to give you a lecture on history; it's to show you how revolutions in film came to be. Because every shift, from silent shorts to CinemaScope epics, from VHS to vertical video, happened because someone challenged the status quo.

Someone asked: *What if we did it differently?* Whether it was the French New Wave rebels or TikTok teens making 15-second horror shorts, change always starts with disruption. And, yes, sometimes that disruption looks like watching a $165 million space opera with no audio and poor-quality brightness on the London

Underground. But even that tells us something. The language of cinema is still evolving. And if you want to be a part of that future - as a filmmaker, cinematographer, or storyteller - you need to understand *why* these shifts happen.

Not just to mourn the loss of big screens but to ask yourself: *What does this mean for how we tell stories now?*

Do we change the types of stories we tell? Should we just give up on cinema cameras and shoot on iPhones instead? Should we come up with a new aspect ratio for iPhones with a dynamic Island notch? I mean, it's a valid question. Technology is dragging us forward whether we like it or not. The tools are getting smaller, cheaper, and more accessible. What used to require a truckload of gear and a 20-person crew can now be done by a teenager in Crocs with a gimbal and a £12 LUT pack. And that's kind of incredible.

But here's the thing: just because the tools evolve doesn't mean the storytelling becomes irrelevant. If anything, it becomes more important. The real challenge is figuring out how to preserve the intention behind the craft and how to keep meaning, emotion, and texture - when everything else around it is changing.

So yes, maybe the audience is watching La La Land on a cracked Android screen while sitting on the loo. That doesn't mean you stop caring about how you light a scene or frame a shot. It means you adapt with intention. You don't just give up and let the algorithms decide everything. You stay rooted in why you picked up a camera in the first place. That's what this chapter, and honestly, this whole book is about. It's about understanding the lineage of the medium so that you can either honour it, disrupt it, or reinvent it completely. But whatever you do, do it with purpose. If you're going to shoot a short film in 9:16 with an iPhone 13, do it because that serves the story, not just because it's trendy.

As of 2025, the average human attention span is approximately 8.25 seconds, a decline from 12 seconds in 2000. This suggests that, on average, humans now have shorter attention spans than goldfish, which are often cited as having a 9-second attention span.

**Generational Differences:**
Gen Z (born 1997–2012): Average attention span of 6–8 seconds.
Millennials (born 1981–1996): Approximately 12 seconds.
Gen X (born 1965–1980): Around 15 seconds.
-Baby Boomers (born 1946–1964): Approximately 20 seconds.
Where It's All Headed

We're entering an era of AI, virtual production (utilizing LED walls, as seen in The Mandalorian), and immersive experiences. A blend of video games, film, and interactivity is on the horizon. But with all this technology, the heart of cinema remains the same: a character, a journey, and a visual language that lets us feel something we can't always express in words.

Film is growing up fast. It's experimenting. It's rebelling again. And that's what makes it so exciting to be part of right now. As a young filmmaker, you're not just part of the industry; you're part of its evolution.

There was a time when filmmaking was an exclusive domain - defined by industry connections, big budgets, and years of climbing the Hollywood ladder. However, in the era of smartphones, YouTube, and democratized tools, the barriers are not just lower— they're dissolving altogether.

**Case in point:** Wesley Wang, a high school senior from Long Island, made a 13-minute short film called "Nothing, except Everything". as his graduation project. It wasn't backed by a studio nor funded by wealthy investors. Instead, he taught chess lessons to support it financially. The film, unusual for a short film, was a little cheesy, but it was his style, and most importantly, it resonated.

It went viral on YouTube, amassing millions of views. But it wasn't just internet fame. That raw, emotional storytelling caught the eye of TriStar Pictures, leading to a feature deal. Notably, the adaptation will be produced by Darren Aronofsky's Protozoa Pictures- yes, the same Aronofsky who made Requiem for a Dream and The Whale.

This isn't just a Cinderella story. It's proof that cinema is undergoing a tectonic shift. The traditional gatekeepers still exist, but they're no longer the only way in. Today, a filmmaker with a compelling idea, some editing software, and the right instincts for digital storytelling can break through. What used to take decades can now happen in a year.

So, how do you actually make use of this information?

Understanding where cinema came from isn't just a flex. It's a compass. When you study how editing evolved from continuity to chaos, you start to see where it might go next. When you realise how every major cinematic movement was a reaction to the thing before it, you begin to anticipate the next one.

German Expressionism → post-war trauma

French New Wave → rebellion against studio polish

Dogme 95 → Rebellion against everything

TikTok? A rebellion against gatekeeping.

**Task:**

Ask yourself: what are people tired of now?

What are audiences craving?

What feels overdone?

What feels underexplored?

The next revolution is already underway; we're in the midst of it, and just like the past, it's being led by people outside the system.

## You're Not Just a Filmmaker Anymore

The term "filmmaker" is too small now. You're a storyteller. An experimenter. A disruptor. You might shoot something today and release it on Instagram. Tomorrow, you're pitching a TV show. Next month, you're in a VR lab scanning your actor's face into Unreal Engine.

And you know what? That's normal now.

If you try to stay in one lane, if you define yourself only as a "DP," or a "screenwriter" or a "director," you're going to feel left behind. The smartest creatives today are fluid. They flow with tech. They pivot with platforms. They adapt without apologising.

So maybe your next project isn't a film. Maybe it's a branded web series. Or a virtual fashion show. Or a TikTok horror short shot in POV. That doesn't make you less of an artist. It makes you dangerous. The future doesn't need perfection. It needs people who experiment faster than the system can stop them.

## The gameplan:

One thing you should take away from the previous pages is that the access to the cinema is open. It's no longer massive studios handing out luck to people anymore; you have the power to create your own luck.

In the evolving landscape of cinema, social media platforms have become powerful tools for filmmakers to showcase their work, gain recognition, and secure professional opportunities. This chapter examines how individuals are leveraging platforms like YouTube, TikTok, and Instagram Reels to advance their filmmaking careers, exploring the balance between luck, skill, and replicable strategies.

Julian Bass, a 20-year-old student, created a TikTok video showcasing his self-taught visual effects skills, transforming into various characters. The video went viral, capturing the attention of Disney executive chairman Bob Iger and resulting in offers from industry professionals.

Can you imagine how hard this would be for someone ten years ago? To get a shot at getting a job at Disney would seem impossible.

Through his consistent work, he has been able to capture the right audience and reach the right people to realise his dream.

Filmmaker Christian Nilsson co-created *Unsubscribe*, a horror film shot over Zoom. By renting out a theater and purchasing all the tickets himself, he propelled the film to the top of the U.S. box office during the COVID-19 pandemic.

This is absolutely unthinkable to even consider. But the takeaway here is that he saw an opportunity and took it. He was aware of the rules and played it to his advantage. Social media is one of the biggest ways people are entering this industry right now, whether it's film, TV, or even commercials.

Let's get this out of the way first: social media is not a magic wand. It won't turn a weak film into an Oscar contender overnight. But when it's used right, it can be an extremely powerful tool for getting your work seen, growing your name, and opening doors you didn't even know existed. You don't need to be an "influencer," and you don't have to dance on TikTok (unless that's your thing). What you do need is a system a smart, creative way to turn your passion into consistent visibility.

## Pick a Platform - But Know What It's For

There's a reason not everyone posts the same thing across Instagram, TikTok, and YouTube: each platform has its own vibe.

- TikTok is the best place for short, weird, funny, high-impact content. It favors authenticity and speed over polish.

- Instagram Reels is a visual storytelling tool — good for mood pieces, micro-narratives, BTS clips, or building your personal filmmaker brand.

- YouTube is for long-form content, behind-the-scenes breakdowns, tutorials, short films, and even vlogs.

- X (Twitter) is great for film discourse, connecting with other filmmakers, and getting the attention of festival programmers, execs, or journalists.

**Tip:** Start with one or two to begin. Don't overwhelm yourself trying to "be everywhere." Focus on where your content fits best.

## Show, Don't Sell

Too many young filmmakers treat social media like LinkedIn. "Looking for work! DM me!" gets scrolled past in 0.2 seconds.

What works? Showing your work.

- Share short scenes or clips from your films.
- Break down lighting setups and transitions.
- Post comparison reels (what you imagined vs. what you shot).
- Tell stories from the set: the chaos, the wins, the accidents that turned into magic.
- Film in-progress experiments. Even the messy ones.

The people who go viral aren't just posting "finished work." They're building a relationship with the audience by inviting them into the *process*.

**Real-World Example:** The director duo at Pickle Pictures on TikTok shares behind-the-scenes (BTS) content and mini-tutorials while creating their own music videos. They rarely ask for work, but their direct messages are full.

## The Content Loop (That Doesn't Burn You Out)

Consistency matters, but you're not a content farm. Here's a weekly system you can actually maintain:

**Week Breakdown:**
- Day 1 (Shoot): Record a mini-scene, a lighting trick, a camera movement breakdown, or set up a tutorial.

- Day 2 (Edit): Chop it up into a 15-30 second Reel/TikTok. Add captions, and keep it punchy.

- Day 3 (Post): Choose the best time your audience is online (usually evenings or lunch hours).

- Day 4 (Engage): Reply to comments, connect with other creatives, and share someone else's work.

- Day 5 (Reflect): What worked? What flopped? Adjust and repeat.

**Bonus Tip:** Batch your content. Shoot 3–4 pieces in one session and schedule them. That way, you're not stuck thinking "What do I post today?" every morning.

## Growing Beyond the Screen

Going viral is not the end goal. The goal is *leverage*. Use your social presence to open real-world doors:

- Add a call-to-action at the end of some videos ("DM if you want to collab" / "Link in bio for my short film").

- Use success as social proof — put "1M+ views on TikTok" in your email signature or pitch deck.

- Reach out to brands, festivals, or musicians who match your aesthetic and offer to collaborate.

Real-World Example: UK-based filmmaker Naomi Anim started by posting intimate TikToks that recreated poetic moments from her scripts. She now directs branded content for local fashion brands who DM'd her because of those videos.

**Also:** document everything. If you're directing a short, record the journey from script to recce to shoot day. Each of those is a separate piece of content. Your career becomes the content, and the content grows your career.

**Tip:** Meta glasses, or any glasses with a camera, are a great way to get behind-the-scenes footage without worrying about it.

## Luck, Timing, and Staying Sane

Let's be honest: some people blow up randomly. One video pops off, and suddenly, they've got producers knocking. But most of the success stories? They were posting for months, sometimes years. The algorithm finally hit the mark, and they were ready when it did.

**Here's what's in your control:**
- The quality and consistency of your work.
- Your engagement with others in your niche.
- Your storytelling voice.

What's not in your control:

- When your video goes viral.

- Whether a producer sees your post and reaches out.

- The algorithm.

So don't chase the algorithm. Chase growth. Learn a little every week. Connect with people. Use your content to refine your voice, not just build followers.

If you do this for 6–12 months consistently, with work you're proud of, something will land. It might be a freelance gig. It might be a festival. It might be a shoutout from someone bigger. But the point is that you're no longer waiting around for permission. You're *building* your own career — one post at a time.

Always remember, the goal is not social media fame; it's to create meaningful, purpose-filled content that inspires you. Don't drift away from your initial goal just because you want to get more work.

One of the biggest shifts in modern filmmaking isn't about tech it's about connection. The myth of the lone genius is fading fast. Today, filmmakers who thrive are the ones who don't just post for likes; they post to build community. They document their process, share their wins and losses, and create an ecosystem where others can learn, engage, and root for them.

This is how you go from "just another filmmaker online" to someone people trust, remember, and want to hire. Community creates momentum. One person might comment on your frame because they love your LUT. Another might DM you, asking to collaborate. Over time, these tiny interactions become your informal network, your tribe. And that's the secret: visibility gets you noticed. Community gets you support for the long-term.

Let's bring it home. How do you actually use this understanding to your advantage? Here's a no-fluff checklist:

**1. Study Movement, Not Just Movies**
Don't just watch films. Watch what changed cinema.
Learn why the French New Wave happened.
Understand what Dogme 95 was reacting to.
Ask what TikTok cinema says about attention spans and why people are resonating with it.

**2. Make Fast, Make Often**
The old model was: Make one perfect film every 3 years.
The new model: make 10 experiments a month.
Publish. Test. Fail. Learn. Repeat.

**3. Design for Platforms**

This one hurts, but it's actually gaining traction. Film call sheets now specify "Vertical Drama."

A hard pill to swallow, but stop fighting the vertical video trend. Embrace it.

Think in aspect ratios. Frame your story for where it lives.

Platforms aren't the enemy. They're amplifiers.

**4. Think Like a Studio, Act Like an Artist**

Learn basic marketing. Know how to write loglines. Cut trailers.

Make your own behind-the-scenes reels.

Understand what makes something shareable and watchable.

You are the creator and distributor.

**5. Stay Curious About Tech**

Don't be scared of AI. Play with it. Use it as a collaborator.

Learn Unreal Engine. Test volumetric video.

Every new tool is a new brush. Paint with it.

Use it to streamline your tasks to increase your output efficiency.

Final Thought: The Future Belongs to the Weirdos

Every film revolution started with someone being told, "That'll never work."

Méliès faking explosions.

Godard is breaking the fourth wall.

Nolan is shooting backward.

Some Gen Z kid is making an entire narrative on Snapchat.

That's your invitation.

You don't need to wait for permission. You just need to make something weird. And make it with heart.

The future of film isn't just about where it's going.

It's about who's brave enough to take it there.

So go on.
Break something.
Fix it differently.
And make the cinema yours.

## Interview Section

In today's film landscape, the tools we use to tell stories aren't just cameras and lights; they're also reels, tutorials, swipe-ups, and comment sections. Social media has changed the game, not just in how films are marketed but in how filmmakers are discovered, educated, and connected. In this ever-evolving digital jungle, one filmmaker who's carved out a powerful presence is Ruben Scott.

Ruben isn't just making films - he's building community. His Instagram page is a blend of cinematic know-how, transparency about the creative process, and a genuine passion for helping other filmmakers grow. While many treat social media as a highlight reel,

Ruben treats it like a classroom, a behind-the-scenes pass, and a conversation all rolled into one.

In this chapter, we sit down for a conversation with Ruben to explore how filmmakers can effectively leverage online platforms without compromising their artistic integrity. We talk about gear, growth, storytelling, and staying grounded while going viral. Whether you're a seasoned DOP or just filmed your first shot on your phone, there's something here for you.

This isn't just about likes or followers - it's about connection, craft, and creating a career that's truly yours.

**Q:** Ruben, your Instagram presence is a treasure trove for filmmakers. What inspired you to start sharing your journey and resources online?

**Ans:** As filmmakers, we're always looking for ways to set ourselves apart in a competitive industry. The filmmaking world is busy, and standing out is crucial. I wanted to grow my social media presence to see where it would lead. I was talking with my brother about the increasing importance of social media, and that conversation inspired me to build an online presence for several reasons:

-To have a space where I can showcase my work and get eyes on it. Often, work in the industry gets lost or overlooked.

-To establish my authority and competence.

-To help me win more work. The more exposure you get, the better.

-To differentiate myself from other filmmakers.

These factors drove me to start growing my social media.

**Q:** You've mentioned the importance of storytelling in your posts. How do you approach storytelling in your projects?

**Ans:** Great question! I focus on telling the stories of good causes. I love working with people and brands that have a purpose to make a positive impact. For example, the WWF's Earth Hour project aimed to encourage people to turn off their lights for an hour to help the planet. For each of my projects, I utilize the Pixar 5-step storytelling structure, which can be easily found online. It helps me refine the story and make sure everything aligns. I constantly ask myself, "Because of that," to keep the story moving forward and make sure it holds together.

**Q:** What advice would you give to aspiring filmmakers looking to build their presence online?

**Ans:** Do it! As I've shared, there are many reasons I started, but creating social media content is also a valuable skill to have as a filmmaker. It teaches you to think about your audience, keep their attention, and eliminate unnecessary details—skills that will directly enhance your filmmaking.

For anyone just starting, I recommend keeping things simple. Pick one platform, decide what your page is about, and ask yourself how it helps people, whether it informs, educates, or entertains. Once you've figured that out, go for it! Developing your style takes time, but the best things are worth the wait.

**Q:** How do you see the role of social media evolving in the film industry?

**Ans:** In the past, people were obsessed with power. Now, the focus is on gaining attention through social media. Social media presence is already influencing casting and hiring decisions. People with larger audiences are more likely to be hired because there's a guaranteed audience once a film is completed.

Over time, this trend will continue to grow. Filmmakers with large followings have an advantage. Even if a filmmaker with fewer followers is slightly more skilled, producers often prefer those with a larger audience. Social media is now another tool in the filmmaker's toolkit.

**Q:** Can you paint us a picture of a memorable experience where your online presence led to a professional opportunity?

**Ans:** Without my social media presence, I'm sure I wouldn't have had the opportunities that came from projects like WWF Earth Hour, Tony's Chocolonely, or Nudie Jeans. Additionally, filmmaking brands like DZOFilm, Aputure, and Nanlite have supported me by loaning and gifting equipment in exchange for social media shoutouts. There's a unique currency in social media, and those opportunities wouldn't have happened without my online presence.

**Q:** What's next for you in your filmmaking journey?

**Ans:** One of the best things about this industry is that we never know what's coming around the corner! One phone call can change everything, so it's hard to predict. At the moment, my production company, Beyond Belief Productions, is wrapping up a project we shot in Amsterdam, which is exciting.

Beyond that, my goals are to continue helping as many people as possible through purposeful brand work and by supporting filmmakers with my social media presence. I love helping people, and I want to expand the scale of everything I do.

**Q:** What are three types of posts that have consistently led to job inquiries or collaborations?

**Ans:** It's tough to narrow it down to just three, but here are the main types of posts that have worked for me:
-Portfolio work that showcases my capabilities.
-Educational content where I share insights or teach about aspects of the filmmaking industry.
-People like to work with those who have knowledge. Content with a unique twist. Something with an interesting angle or perspective that people haven't heard before. When everyone is looking one way, look the other!

**Q:** How do you stay consistent without feeling like you're turning into a 'content creator' more than a filmmaker?

**Ans:** Filmmaking has always been a huge part of my identity. Sharing my filmmaking journey on social media actually makes me feel more like a filmmaker. Occasionally, I remind myself of the "why" behind growing my social media presence and how it benefits me. It's easy to lose sight of the bigger picture, so I focus on the end goal and work backward to understand what's worth doing in the present. Social media is like checking on a plant to see if it's grown—sometimes, the progress is slow, but it's happening!

**Q:** What's something you learned late in your journey that you wish someone told you earlier?

**Ans:** I wish someone had told me to think about my Ikigai earlier. Ikigai is a Japanese concept that helps you discover your purpose, not just in work but in life. It's about finding the intersection of what you love, what you're good at, what the world needs, and what you can be paid for.

When I applied this framework, I realized my Ikigai is telling the stories of purposeful people and brands. I love helping others; I'm passionate about creativity, and I'm skilled at using film to tell stories, which I can monetize. Once I understood my Ikigai, everything I do feels purposeful, and filmmaking no longer feels like just a job to pay the bills.

I'd encourage anyone reading this to find your Ikigai. It'll give you a sense of direction and purpose in everything you do.

## The change being made in Production Companies

Major players, such as Warner Bros., Disney, and Sony, are already investing heavily in AI tools. Warner Bros., for instance, is using AI to help greenlight projects by analysing scripts and predicting box office success. Disney's been experimenting with software that can blend multiple takes to create the perfect performance. Sony, meanwhile, is exploring AI-powered virtual production that renders complex scenes in real-time.

All of these point to a future where AI is part of the creative toolkit, not a gimmick, but a genuine asset. Before getting started, I need to address the concerns about AI, specifically its potential to replace creative roles.

Beyond writing, directors and other creatives worry that AI's ability to automate tasks might diminish the need for human input, potentially leading to job losses and a homogenization of content. There is also concern that AI-generated content, trained on existing works, may lack originality and emotional depth.

What I feel people are missing out on while looking at this is control. We control AI, and does what we tell it (unless we get to ex machina level and build a mind of its own). AI doesn't replace, but rather, it creates agency for us to discover new techniques and avenues to expand our work. Where we spent hours building a call sheet by plugging in each crew member's name, AI can fill that in instantly, giving us more time to focus on the creative aspects. This is what AI lacks - it has no soul and no creativity; it's we who instill that creativity. His is one thing that can't be taught. How do you teach an intangible emotion to a robot?

At times like this, what matters most is controlling how AI is used.

We're starting to see unions and guilds step in, trying to figure out where AI fits in and how to protect human creatives in the process. But one thing's clear: the industry is already in motion, and the conversation isn't about whether AI will be used in film - it's about how we use it.

A few months ago, I was helping a friend with a short film - a low-budget, tight-schedule project, the usual chaos. We were in pre-production, juggling shot lists location permits, and trying to lock in our shooting schedule. My friend had been experimenting with AI tools, and to be honest, I was sceptical.

But then he opened up this AI scheduling tool (nothing fancy, just a free beta he found online), and within five minutes, it had scanned the script, broken down every scene, and proposed a draft shooting schedule based on daylight hours, location availability, and even predicted weather. I was blown away. I sat there thinking, "This just saved us three days of stress and sticky notes."

It didn't take my job away, but it definitely made my job easier. Even smaller studios and indie filmmakers are catching on, using AI for everything from editing and color grading to visual effects and even rough script drafts. It's becoming more accessible by the day, breaking down barriers that once made high-end production feel out of reach for low-budget creators.

I wanted to understand how this was being used by big studios because this would completely shift the way that people recruit for jobs. Apart from the things I noticed companies adopting, I've also outlined ways you can take advantage of these implementations.

## 1. AI in Scriptwriting and Pre-Production

Script Analysis: Studios like 20th Century Fox have utilised AI tools such as ScriptBook to analyse scripts, predicting box office success and providing insights into plot and character development.

If you're a screenwriter or script consultant, learn how to use these tools to get instant feedback on your scripts. Being able to interpret AI-generated insights and refine your work based on those will position you as a writer who's both creative and data-savvy. You can even offer script analysis as a service to production companies.

**Greenlighting Decisions:** Warner Bros. partnered with Cinelytic to assess the potential success of a film. Cinelytic analyzes a wealth of historical data, including film descriptions, casting choices, and release strategies, allowing studios to make data-driven decisions. For example, suppose the studio wants to test how Scarlett Johansson in a lead role would affect box office revenue. In that case, they can input the data and get a prediction on potential returns in various markets.

However, while these AI tools can predict success based on patterns in historical data, they don't always provide deep insights. For instance, it's not groundbreaking to say that a movie with Tom Cruise or a big summer action film will likely perform well at the box office. One limitation is that these AI tools are based on past data, meaning they could reinforce existing patterns, such as undiverse casting choices, thus perpetuating Hollywood's lack of diversity. Warner Bros. intends to primarily utilize AI for marketing and distribution rather than for the creative aspects of film production.

**How People Can Take Advantage of This:** Data-Driven Insight Providers: People with a background in data analysis or AI can position themselves as consultants or strategists for film studios. By understanding how AI predicts movie success, you can offer valuable insights on audience targeting and marketing strategies, making you a valuable asset in the growing intersection between film and technology.

Marketing Professionals: If you're in marketing or social media, gaining expertise in AI tools for film promotion (like Cinelytic's audience targeting features) can set you apart. Studios are using AI to determine which trailers, posters, and campaigns will resonate most with specific demographics. Learning how to optimize campaigns using this data will make you an appealing candidate for positions within these studios.

Creative Professionals: While AI won't replace creative decisions, writers, producers, and directors can leverage data insights to gain a deeper understanding of market trends and audience preferences. Understanding how to utilize AI tools for pre-production or post-production marketing decisions can open up new opportunities in Hollywood's evolving landscape.

In conclusion, Warner Bros.' focus on AI is shaping the future of film marketing. By developing skills in AI-based tools for marketing and data analysis, you can position yourself at the forefront of the industry's shift toward more data-driven decision-making.

## 2. AI in Post-Production

**De-Ageing and Face Replacement:** The film "Here" employed Metaphysic's generative AI to de-age actors Tom Hanks and Robin Wright in real-time during filming, eliminating the need for extensive post-production work.

**Emotion Synthesis**: Disney's FaceDirector software enables the blending of different facial expressions from multiple takes, thereby enhancing emotional continuity in scenes.

**Crowd Simulation:** AI tools, such as Massive Software, have been utilized to generate realistic crowd scenes, as seen in Ant-Man and the Wasp: Quantumania.

**Automated Editing:** Adobe's Sensei uses machine learning to automate tasks such as object removal and scene stabilization, reducing editing time.

**Sound Categorisation:** Skywalker Sound employs AI to categorize and retrieve sounds from its vast library, streamlining the sound design process.

**Trailer Creation:** IBM Watson was used to creating the trailer for the film Morgan, analysing visuals and sounds to determine the most appealing content for audiences.

Phew, I know this is a lot of information and so many new software programs you might not have heard about yet.

How You Can Position Yourself: If you're an editor, learning how to use these AI-powered tools will allow you to drastically speed up your workflow while maintaining a high level of quality. You can market yourself as an editor who leverages AI to streamline tedious tasks and deliver top-notch results more efficiently. Additionally, AI can handle repetitive tasks, such as syncing sound or matching shots, allowing you to focus on more complex creative decisions.

You get the gist of how AI is being widely used by these companies; they're really going all in.

## Case Studies

The Brutalist faced criticism for using AI to enhance actors' Hungarian dialogue, raising questions about authenticity and AI's role in

**Emilia Pérez:** An example of AI's growing presence in award-nominated films, indicating its increasing acceptance in mainstream cinema. The integration of AI in major film studios marks a significant shift in the filmmaking landscape. While it offers numerous advantages in efficiency and creativity, it also presents challenges that require careful consideration. As the industry continues to evolve, striking a balance between innovation and tradition will be crucial.

# Chapter 6 - Coming to a close

Circling back again to the core of this book, instilling the love of cinema and showing ways of thriving in this industry to people who dream of being leaders in this beautiful craft. Film is beautiful; it's a blend of literature, music, visuals, performance, fashion, and architecture all in one. It's a burst of creative energy that people in this world get to experience. Don't lose track of this power of cinema; it has the power to change. I've seen it, and if you look closely, you will see it too. Films influence everyone around you; life is not a film, and it's not a metaphor for anything. Everyone wishes that the magic of film bleeds into their life.

So, for everyone who has reached the end of this book, I can speak for my generation of filmmakers who are battling with uncertainty, pushing ahead to create a new era of filmmaking—to keep cinema alive. London is a city that, when you live there, might seem cold and hostile, and everyone seems distant. However, one thing that is common in all of my shoots is that I meet at least one person on the crew that I have worked with before. It's a small world, and we're all in this together.

Use this book as your diary of powering ahead through this storm. Don't lose your light, no matter how hard it gets, and no matter if no one's watching - you be your own supporter. But know that if you need support, it's just one call away. We're all one big, sometimes dysfunctional, chaotic family of misfits that just show up with the same creative energy as day one. I hope my writing has taught you at least one thing. I promise to keep learning, growing, and writing to keep this craft alive. I love cinema, how much do you?

# Bibliography

**Books & Essays**

- Goldman, William. Adventures in the Screen Trade. Warner Books, 1983.

- Murch, Walter. In the Blink of an Eye: A Perspective on Film Editing. Silman-James Press, 2001.

- Rodriguez, Robert. Rebel Without a Crew. Dutton, 1995.

- Mamet, David. On Directing Film. Penguin, 1992.

- Glebas, Francis. Directing the Story. Focal Press, 2008.

- Rabiger, Michael, and Hurbis-Cherrier, Mick. Directing: Film Techniques and Aesthetics. Routledge, 6th Edition, 2020.

- Hoffman, Reid. Impromptu: Amplifying Our Humanity Through AI. 2023.

- Nichols, Bill. Introduction to Documentary. Indiana University Press, 2010.

## Industry Guides / UK-Specific

- British Film Institute (BFI). *Statistical Yearbook* and industry reports. www.bfi.org.uk.

- ScreenSkills. *Entry Routes and Career Maps.* www.screenskills.com.

- Film London. *Breaking into Film & TV.* .www.filmlondon.org.uk.

## Articles & Whitepapers

- Variety & Deadline articles on trends in UK production.

- *The Future of Filmmaking in a Virtual Production Era*, Unreal Engine, Epic Games.

- *Cinematography in the Digital Age*, American Cinematographer Magazine.

- *AI Tools in Pre-Production and Storyboarding*, No Film School, 2023.

## Podcasts

- *Team Deakins* (Hosted by Roger and James Deakins).

- *The Wandering DP Podcast* (Hosted by Patrick O'Sullivan).

- *The Business* (KCRW – Hosted by Kim Masters).

- *The No Film School Podcast.*

## Websites & Platforms

- ScreenSkills – Career guides, CV help, and industry-endorsed training.

- BFI – Funding opportunities, festivals, and research.

- The Mandy Network – Job listings for the crew.

- Shooting People – Networking for indie filmmakers.

- Film & TV Charity – Mental health and financial support for UK creatives.

- ProductionBase – Industry-standard job listings.

www.ingramcontent.com/pod-product-compliance
Lightning Source LLC
Chambersburg PA
CBHW050734010526
44107CB00010B/849